THANKS BE TO GOD: A MINISTER'S MEMOIR

GRATITUDE AND SPIRITUAL JOURNEY

LARRY LAPIERRE

Thanks Be To God: A Minister's Memoir
Gratitude and Spiritual Journey
Copyright © 2019 by Larry LaPierre

All rights reserved. No part of this publication may be reproduced, distributed, or transmitted in any form or by any means, including photocopying, recording, or other electronic or mechanical methods, without the prior written permission of the publisher or author, except in the case of brief quotations embodied in critical reviews and certain other noncommercial uses permitted by copyright law.

Although every precaution has been taken to verify the accuracy of the information contained herein, the author and publisher assume no responsibility for any errors or omissions. No liability is assumed for damages that may result from the use of information contained within.

Library of Congress Control Number: 2019938045
ISBN-13:   Paperback: 978-1-950073-11-5
           PDF: 978-1-950073-12-2
           ePub: 978-1-950073-13-9
           Kindle: 978-1-950073-14-6

Printed in the United States of America

GoToPublish LLC
1-888-337-1724
www.gotopublish.com
info@gotopublish.com

Contents

ACKNOWLEDGEMENTS V

PERMISSION VII

DEDICATION IX

PREFACE XI

INTRODUCTION XV

PRELUDE—TWO VITAL STORIES XIX

CHAPTER 1—FAMILY 1

CHAPTER 2—FRIENDS 17

CHAPTER 3—MENTORS 41

CHAPTER 4—TEACHERS OF ALL KINDS 55

CHAPTER 5—COLLEAGUES IN MINISTRY 77

CHAPTER 6—PARISHIONERS 89

CHAPTER 7—VETERANS AND HOSPITAL STAFF 105

CONCLUSION 117

ACKNOWLEDGEMENTS

This entire book is a series of acknowledgements of people who have been instrumental in my growth. I owe them more than this small book can ever adequately describe. I believe that God worked through each of them to help me become the person that I am.

PERMISSION

New Revised Standard Version Bible, copyright 1989, Division of Christian Education of the National Council of the Churches of Christ in the United States of America. Used by permission. All rights reserved.

© Lawrence L. LaPierre   (November 28, 2009)

76 Quail Hollow Drive, San Jose, CA 95128-4534

cirrider@att.net

DEDICATION

This book is dedicated to the three women who have made the greatest impact on my life:

Dorothy—My mother

Jane—My wife

Laura—Our daughter

PREFACE

This book is a memoir. It is not a history of my life. Instead, it is a selection of stories based upon what I can remember and, frankly, on what I believe would be helpful to reveal.

My intent is to acknowledge with gratitude many of the people who have made a positive difference in my life. There have been quite a number of them and I am grateful for each person who has given me the gift that she or he had to give. Your gift wasn't always acknowledged by me at the time. Sometimes I didn't even appreciate it until years later.

However, I am not only grateful to you for what you did for me. I am also grateful to God for sending you into my life and making it possible for me to learn or to otherwise receive what you gave me. A friend once said to me, "Larry, there are no coincidences in life." I believe that. When I have crossed paths with a person, even if it has been only for a few minutes, God has been present to enable me to learn or to otherwise receive whatever was being offered to help me to grow as a person.

A simple example, which is not recorded elsewhere in this book, involves a young woman whom I met at Northeastern University in Boston around 1972. I remember that we were both standing outside one of the university buildings and I remember that she seemed to be a few years younger than me. It's what she said that made an impact on me. She told me a story of how she had been married to a captain in the United States Army and how, not long before, he had been killed in Vietnam. I had not, as far as I knew, met a widow of a war veteran—certainly not one so young. She allowed me to hear and perhaps to feel a little of the price that she and her husband, among many others, paid in the Vietnam War. It may have helped me to be a better Veterans Affairs chaplain when it came time to serve in that capacity.

But why did I write this book? It is not simply because I am grateful for all the help that I've been given over my lifetime. It is specifically because of what the Troy Annual Conference of The United Methodist Church did the year that I retired (2004). Up to that point retiring pastors had been given an opportunity to address the Annual Conference (a yearly meeting of pastors and laity who represented the churches that belonged to the Troy Annual Conference). In 2004, however, it was decided that retiring pastors would be invited to come to a conference location and be interviewed for an hour. The interview would be recorded on video. Then three minutes of that hour-long interview would be selected to play at the Annual Conference meeting instead of allowing the retiring pastors to speak. I can barely list the locations of the churches that I've served in three minutes! Worse yet, I wouldn't even get to select what was played at the Annual Conference from the interview.

So, this book is born out of a need to say much more than can be said in three minutes. It is also born out of a need to look back at my life and examine some of the ways that God has blessed me through the lives and love of many, many people.

If you know me and don't find your name or your story recorded here it is not because I don't value what you did for me. Not at all! It may be that I have forgotten. I am sorry to say that my memory is not what it used to be. It is also possible that I wanted to protect either my privacy or yours.

You whose contributions appear in this book, as well as those of you who are not described in these pages, gave me far more than I can ever describe. I literally wouldn't be the person that I am today without you. Thank you all and may God bless each of you!

Larry LaPierre

INTRODUCTION

Like most people, my life has been a mixture of good and bad experiences. Over thirty years ago a social worker asked me how I had escaped the impact that growing up in a dysfunctional family had had on my brother and sister. The truth was that I hadn't escaped. However, "The rest of the story," as Paul Harvey used to say, is that I knew that my life had been made much easier because of several people who helped me at critical points in my life.

Who are these people? Many of them are the people around whom I have written this memoir. Their stories shed light on how my life was shaped by people who may never have realized what a difference they have made.

This book is one way of saying "Thank You" to many of these people. I will refer to most of them by their first names to protect their privacy.

My appreciation for the difference each of these people has made in my life is best summed up in a comment made by one of my seminary professors. When someone complimented him on a book that he had written, Dr. Burton Throckmorton humbly stated, "We stand on each other's shoulders."

I believe that. I believe that all of us are better for having met at least some of the people in our lives—perhaps many. I also know that we need those people both to help us know that we belong to a caring community and to help us to cope with our brokenness.

Brokenness in human lives takes a number of forms. It might be a physical brokenness like a broken back that keeps us from walking. We might live with an emotional condition that makes it difficult for us to trust people. We might even live with a psychiatric condition that drives us from the depths of despondency to exuberant behavior that challenges the limits of common sense and safety. Or we may be left with a broken relationship such as a divorce or having been ostracized by our family. We may also experience brokenness because we feel condemned by God or whatever our Higher Power is.

Brokenness can gradually develop in our lives as we live in a dysfunctional family. The people around us teach us, by their example, how to live a dysfunctional lifestyle. We, in turn, teach those lessons to others. I come from one such family and I have lived, to varying degrees over the decades, a dysfunctional life.

Obviously, there are many reasons why people feel "broken." Sometimes it is because of what we have done that is hurtful to ourselves or to others. However, it helps to know that at least some of what doesn't work well about us is not because we are bad people or willfully difficult to live with. It is because of what we have endured or what we have needed and not been given.

My earliest memory of this reality goes back to sometime when I was in my early twenties. I remember nothing about the circumstances other than I was at work and I got angry. Someone accused me of overreacting.

I responded, "You wouldn't say that if you had been through what I have been through!" At the time I didn't realize why I said that.

Nevertheless, most of us are responsible for doing what we can to heal from our brokenness. One way that I began to heal was opened for me when people taught me about God. They helped me to believe that God loved me. In later years I continue to be helped and even challenged to grow by other people whom God sends to me.

Some of you may not believe in God. If you do believe in God you may not be able to believe that God sends people into our lives to help us. Perhaps Nature is your Higher Power. Or you belong to a religion in which there is no God or other Higher Power. Still others may want me to understand that the universe and what happens to us is utterly unpredictable.

Whatever our beliefs about the role God or another Higher Power has or has not played in our lives, I hope that we can recognize that we are not solely responsible for who we have become. Others have played a role in shaping us. Some have made our lives more difficult. Others have helped. Even those who have made our lives more difficult may have helped us to develop ways to cope.

In reading my stories perhaps you will be inspired to remember people who have helped you to heal, to grow and to achieve more than you ever thought possible. If you can remember such people give thanks. Consider also that you may be called to help others as many have helped you.

PRELUDE
—TWO VITAL STORIES

Without the people involved in these two stories, the rest of my life might have been very different.

It was 1949 and my mother, my sister and I had arrived in Germany to join my father who was stationed in Berlin as part of the American Army of occupation. We were traveling at night on a train that was taking us from Bremerhaven to Berlin. I woke up sometime during the night. The train had stopped and I could hear men's voices. The next morning the conductor told my mother that the East German police had tried to take us off the train. They had claimed that our papers were not made out correctly. I have often wondered what my life would have been like if the East German police had succeeded in getting us off of the train. Would I have been forced to grow up in the East German Communist nation? Would I have become a Communist? Or would our family have simply been detained for awhile in the struggle between the Communist nations and the West? It was one of those roads not taken and I am grateful that the conductor was able to keep us from being taken off of that train.

The second story happened during the Vietnam War. It was 1966 and I had just quit college. It is a long story as to why it happened but the bottom line was that I didn't think that I could cope with all of the pressures in my life at that time. However, I also knew that by quitting college I would soon be drafted and, once drafted, I stood a very high chance of going to Vietnam.

I decided to volunteer for the Army and I got on a bus with a lot of other young men to go for the Army physical in Springfield, Massachusetts. I passed the physical exam. There was just one more doctor to see. He asked me if there was anything that I had not told the other doctors.

I said that I had had a duodenal ulcer three years earlier, that it had not bled and that it was not causing me any problems. I was simply answering his question. I had no thought that it would have any bearing on joining the army. However, the doctor said, "You're out of here." I asked why. He said that if I got into situations of high stress, such as combat, that the ulcer was likely to come back. I left not knowing what to feel. Two weeks later I was notified that I was rated as 4F—unsuitable for service in the military. It was not a proud moment in my life because my father had served twenty-three years in the United States Army.

Later, when I served as a Department of Veterans Affairs chaplain I learned something about what might have happened to me if I had not been rated 4F. For one thing, I might have been killed in Vietnam. Over fifty-eight thousand Americans were killed in Vietnam and many more were injured. Many of those injured lived with permanent disabilities. As a chaplain who led spirituality groups and did some one-to-one counseling I learned that there are a lot of disabling conditions that one cannot see in a veteran's body. They are nevertheless very real and often affect the person's mind or spirit. Sometimes a veteran is so badly damaged emotionally and/or spiritually that s/he is unable to maintain loving relationships either with people or with God. All of that I escaped by being rated 4F.

That doctor at the Army examination center may have saved my life. He almost certainly saved me from a lot of suffering. I doubt that I would have been emotionally healthy enough to be a loving husband and father if I had been in combat. On the other hand, I recognize that someone else took my place and I regret whatever he endured. I gladly served twelve years as a VA chaplain to help the veterans in whatever ways I could.

CHAPTER 1
—FAMILY

My Parents' Families:

Perhaps every family of origin is dysfunctional to some degree. It helps me to know that my family's problems began with the experience of earlier generations. I never knew until the year before my father died that his father had beaten his sons with a bullwhip. The emotional and perhaps spiritual scars that those beatings left on my father and his three brothers must have been immense and longer lasting than the physical damage. One of my father's sisters was repeatedly abused by her husband and his other sister died as a result of being brought home in bitterly cold weather too soon after giving birth to my cousin. One of the ways that my father coped with his emotional pain was to drink so much that he became an alcoholic. Another was to be violent at times.

My mother's family suffered enormous losses due to death and poverty. Her mother had ten babies and six of them were either born dead or died within the first year of birth. My mother's father died when she was seven years old from pneumonia. It was 1927 and there were no antibiotics. Her mother died in 1938 when my mother was eighteen years old. It was the time known as The Great Depression and her family had already lived on welfare for years.

My Father:

Both of my parents had a great influence on me. When I was young my father's influence on me seemed to be entirely negative. Yet he did teach me some lessons that have helped me. When we were working around the house or out in the barn he would remind me, "If you don't learn how to fix things yourself you'll have to pay someone else to do it." So I learned to do a lot of what needed to be done to keep a home in good repair and a car running.

My father also taught me to love flowers. It's not that I've ever been such a great gardener. But I did have a period when I photographed a lot of flowers with a macro (close up) lens. I still find a great deal of pleasure in looking at flowers.

A third lesson that my father taught me was to mean what I say. He believed that you shouldn't tell somebody to do something unless you really meant it. That included being willing to follow through on whatever you said. I tried never to say anything to our children that I didn't mean. There were no false promises of punishment or vague threats of privileges being withheld if they didn't comply with what I said. There were likewise no false promises of rewards if they complied with our wishes. That carried over into my professional life as a chemist, a pastor and later as a hospital chaplain. I never wanted to say more than what I believed to be true whether it was at a meeting, while preaching a sermon or when answering a dying veteran's question about whether there was hope of eternal peace for her or for him.

My dad also believed in protecting his family. I knew from an early age that he would give his life for us. As far as I know there was never a time when that resolve was tested. But the message was there for me. I was to do whatever was necessary to protect my family.

One of the ways in which my father demonstrated his commitment to his extended family was told to me by two of his nephews—Bill and Bob. They were the sons of his older sister Florence and they came to my father's funeral in 1962. I knew from comments that my father made that his older sister had endured quite a lot of abuse from her husband. Both Bill and Bob confirmed that reality without my asking. They shared with me how, when things were going badly at their home, that my father would come to New York City and "straighten things out" and life would be OK for awhile. I never knew for certain but I suspect that my father used force to make his brother-in-law stop abusing his older sister and their children. Whatever he did, my cousins were grateful for my father's help.

My father also taught me to work hard. He did that by his example. After he retired from the army he worked as what is known as a boiler fireman. This is a person who is in charge of operating a high pressure steam boiler to supply power to some sort of factory. My father worked fifty-six hours a week at his job and then would come home and work on a garden or do repairs around the house.

One of the more remarkable stories about my father involved his attitude toward a Roman Catholic priest in a nearby parish. The priest was known as Father D. I had seen him a few times but thought little more than that he seemed to be a gentle person. My father, who had little use for church after a confrontation he had around 1953 with another priest, spoke highly of Father D. In fact, he was one of only a very few people that I ever heard my father speak kindly and respectfully about. Father D.

later went on to have a ministry of healing that was well-known in central and eastern Massachusetts and perhaps beyond.

A lesson that my father taught me that may have transcended all of the other lessons was that it was OK for a man to cry. You need to understand that my father was one of the strongest, toughest and, at times, meanest men I have ever met. It is also important to know that I only saw him cry when he was drunk. Even so, it made a great impression on me. He freed me to cry especially when the emotional or spiritual pain was overwhelming.

A final story about the lessons that my father taught me reflects the distance that there was between him and me. I had feared and hated my father for many years because of the abuse that he heaped on our family—despite his willingness to protect us from outside threats. I said something to him that was mean-spirited shortly before he died. Knowing that he could not strike back at me because he was too weak he said, "Go ahead; take your pound of flesh." It is a reference to Shakespeare's play Hamlet. It was also a lesson that I never forgot. It is not fair to say or do something unkind ever but it is especially wrong when a person cannot defend themselves.

My Mother:

Perhaps the greatest lesson that I learned from my mother was that, in every situation, there is always hope. She actually expressed that to me one day when I was at a turning point in my life. I was weeping over an anticipated loss and she said to me, "While there's life there's hope." Years later, when I was reading the Bible, I found a verse that seems to support what she said. It's in Romans 8:28 where St. Paul wrote, "We know that all things work together for good for those who love God, who are called according to his purpose." (NRSV) In other words, even in the worst of situations God is working to bring good into our lives.

Another great gift that my mother gave to me was her stories about being a Protestant. My father was Roman Catholic and we were raised as Catholics. My mother converted to Catholicism around 1950 due to pressure from my father. Yet she spoke from time to time of having been a Methodist when she was a girl. She also told us that she had attended and sung in the choir of a Universalist church when she was older. In fact, my parents were married in that Universalist church in Leominster, Massachusetts.

My mother's background in Protestant churches opened the door for me in 1965 to become involved in the ecumenical movement that began with the Second Vatican Council of the Roman Catholic Church in the 1960s. From that experience came such an appreciation for what the various Protestant traditions had to offer that I was able to do what others might have thought was unthinkable. I dared to leave the Catholic Church in 1973. When I asked my mother how she felt about that she gave me her blessing.

Another liberating story from my mother had to do with her wedding. She told my sister and me that the minister who officiated at her marriage to my father had been a woman. That isn't so surprising in the 21st century but it was a rare situation indeed in 1941. Years later, when I met the first woman minister that I had ever known it never occurred to me that this was anything but normal. For a man raised in the Roman Catholic tradition where only men are ordained, it should have been a shock. A few months later, when I enrolled at Bangor Theological Seminary, I met a number of women who were studying to become clergy. Again, because of my mother's story it never occurred to me that there was anything unusual about meeting women students in a seminary.

Another lesson from my mother was a real help to me as our children got older. She had told me when I was a teenager that she had begun telling herself when my sister and I were quite young that we would grow up and leave home. When our own children left home for college or to go to work at age eighteen it was no surprise to me. I was ready for the change because of what my mother had said.

A lesson that my mother taught me about grief is one that I have continued to use as a minister. It happened not long after my youngest brother died (as a newborn). I asked her if it (the loss) ever stopped hurting. She said, "No, it just hurts less with time." It was a lesson that I was not offered in seminary and I'm glad that my mother helped me to learn it.

A final lesson from my mother had to do with her store of pithy sayings. One that I often use to cope with whatever is going wrong in my life is this: "These things happen in the best of families." Of course things go wrong in every family and it helps to acknowledge that bad things are a normal part of life. However, it was the last phrase that has often enabled me to see humor in situations that were otherwise frustrating. To acknowledge that problems occur "in the best of families" was somehow liberating for we knew that we were not among the "best of families."

Aunt Mabel

Aunt Mabel was my mother's aunt. She was my maternal grandmother's sister. I remember thinking that Aunt Mabel was old when I was a child. She wasn't really that old then but she lived well into her nineties.

I remember her for various reasons but especially because she was still singing at age eighty-eight. I never heard her sing but she told my wife and me that someone from the Grange would pick her up and bring her to a meeting where she would sing.

I also remember her for being very supportive of my decision in 1963 to go out to Minnesota to begin my studies for the Roman Catholic priesthood. When I came back five months later she never questioned or criticized me. In fact, she was one of the people who helped my mother to organize our wedding reception a few years later.

Uncle Red:

My mother's next older brother was named Albourne. However, when my father met him he renamed him "Red" because of the color of his hair. Uncle Red was a quiet although anxious man. His great contribution to my life was to visit us on Thanksgiving and Christmas. He would always come the night before the holiday and stay overnight. We looked forward to having dinner with him the next day and, on Christmas Eve, to opening presents with him.

Uncle Red was one of the islands of sanity in an otherwise tumultuous life as a child. Although he was anxious his presence with our family was somehow a calming presence. He cared about my mother and about us. In dysfunctional families like ours it is not uncommon to assume that the rest of the world is as bizarre as your family is. Uncle Red's presence said that there was more to life than alcoholism, fighting, abuse and depression. There were people outside our immediate dysfunctional family who cared.

Uncle Wendell:

Another uncle who made that point was my mother's oldest brother. He was ten years older than her. Uncle Wendell was a veteran of over three years of combat duty in the South Pacific during World War II. I have many good memories of him. He told stories of his time in the South Pacific but they were either funny stories or accounts of his non-combat duties during the war. He never spoke of the horrors of combat although he alluded to being in desperate situations on occasion.

He opened my eyes to the existence of a way of life that I had never even read about with his stories about life on the island of Borneo. He told me of seeing women there who were about to give birth as the tribe was climbing through the mountains. These women would leave the tribe and go into the bush to give birth to their babies. Half an hour later the women would rejoin the tribe with their babies. This contrasted sharply to the stories that I heard from my mother about women being in the hospital for ten days at the time when I was born.

Uncle Wendell was another man, like his brother Uncle Red, who modeled sanity for us. He, too, would come to visit on the holidays and provide another presence in our lives. This may not sound like very much of a contribution to you who are reading this book but we had essentially no other company when we were young.

One story from my early childhood that involved Uncle Wendell stands out. It was just after World War II and I must have been four or five years old. I was playing with a boy from the house next door named John. I must have gotten upset with him because I raised my cap gun and was either about to hit him with it or actually did hit him. My Uncle Wendell was nearby and he immediately stopped me from hitting John. He wasn't violent but he was quite determined that I would stop my assault. Uncle Wendell taught me more about not hurting other people in that one incident than I would learn for many years.

As I grew older Uncle Wendell taught me about fishing. That included ice fishing during the winter at the pond owned by the Leominster Sportsmen's Club where we were both members. One memorable experience that I had during an ice fishing derby occurred in January during the early 1960s when I stepped into a hole in the ice and sank the full length of my right leg into the frigid waters. There were people all around but no one noticed what had happened. I pulled myself out of the water and stood up. Even as I stood up I could feel my pants freezing as the water rapidly turned to ice. I found my uncle and told him what happened. In his typically understated way he suggested that I should probably go home to change my clothes. Indeed. He didn't overreact and neither did I.

Uncle Wendell also taught me an important lesson about helping people. He told me about stopping to help someone who had a flat tire. After changing the tire the man whom he had helped offered Uncle Wendell some money. My uncle refused the money saying, "Help someone else when you have the opportunity."

Once I began to drive I would visit him at the Sportsmen's Club where he eventually became the caretaker. When I was old enough we would share a beer and he would tell stories while I listened. One day he said something about God that has been important to me ever since. Now he knew that I was a good Catholic man who went to church every Sunday. I knew that he was a good man who did not go to church at all as far as I knew. On this particular day over forty-five years ago he pointed over to the woods and said, "Anytime that I want to talk with God I walk into the woods and talk with him there." Years later that would form the basis of one of my spirituality assessment questions to the veterans I met in the VA hospital in Vermont: "Do you find a sense of peace in Nature?" Like my Uncle Wendell almost every one of them acknowledged that they did.

Jane:

Jane and I were married on January 28, 1967 in what she describes as a Gothic cathedral. It was an immense Roman Catholic church that probably seated fifteen hundred people. Certainly it was much larger than the average Protestant church.

There were only a few dozen of us in the church that snowy January day. Yet it was the most important day of my life. I loved Jane then and I love her even more now. However, on that day and only on that day, I could feel my knees shaking as she walked down the aisle. I was overwhelmed with joy that she was willing to marry me but I must have also been feeling anxious about the commitment that I was about to make.

We had three children all of whom are married and living amazingly productive, successful lives. We have two wonderful daughters-in-law, one great son-in-law, three very special grandchildren and several nieces and nephews. They have all been generous with their love for us and they are all remarkable people. I never envisioned what a wonderful family we would have and I give thanks to God and to Jane for making our family possible.

I would not be the person that I am if it were not for Jane. Her love has been unconditional and she has helped me to understand what it means to love unconditionally. She has supported me through three careers, four degrees, thirteen geographic moves and two significantly disabling conditions. I could not ask for a more loving, supportive and forgiving wife and mother of our children.

Our Older Son:

Our older son helped me to learn a number of lessons. One of them concerned church. He really wanted to be in worship on Sundays when I was pastoring in north-central Maine. However, he worked late on Saturday night and then he stayed out even later with his friends. Hence, he would arrive at the 10:30 a.m. service without enough rest. Despite his best efforts his head would often roll back and he would fall asleep. Nor was he the only one who fell asleep during worship. However, he was the one who helped me to learn that there are reasons why people are sometimes not able to focus on worship. It is one in a long list of lessons that I had to learn after seminary.

He taught me another vital lesson. It was around 1981 and our nation was still in the midst of the Cold War with the Soviet Union. Our older son came home one day from eighth grade and told me that he and his friends did not expect to grow up. When I asked why he said that it was because they expected that there would be a nuclear war before that happened. I was shocked into realizing how threatening the political and military environment was to our young people.

He also demonstrated great courage in the middle of his senior year. I had asked for and had been given a transfer to a church in Vermont. I knew that it would be difficult on our children but I felt it was the right thing to do. He decided to stay in Maine. He did what he needed to do to support himself and he graduated from high school on time.

After graduating from high school our older son went to work instead of directly to college. He worked physically hard for years and endured working conditions that would have been very difficult, perhaps impossible, for me to endure. Finally, he decided to go to college. He earned a bachelor's and master's degree in social work and works as a therapist.

Along the way he helped me to talk about some of my shortcomings as a parent and particularly my problem with listening. It wasn't easy for either of us but I'm glad that we were able to talk about it.

His parenting skills as well as his capacity for hard work and compassion amaze me. He and his wife, Brigitte, raised two wonderful children (Zachory and Jamie). His cooking skills are a tribute to his mother and to his own hard work.

Our Daughter

I suspect that many pastors ignore how adult-centered the average worship service is. However, I was not allowed to be one of them. Our daughter let me know that there were times when she was truly bored with worship as a youngster. She shared with me one of her ways of coping. I was in my first year of seminary and we were attending a United Methodist Church near the seminary. The pastor of that church tended to pray for everybody that he could think of during his pastoral prayer. Our daughter timed his prayers. One day he went way over the line as far as she was concerned. She told me that he had prayed for thirteen minutes. That was when I learned that a pastoral prayer needed to have limits. Her message was later reinforced by the professor who taught the course about prayer at the seminary.

Since her teenage years she has continued to teach me lessons about endurance and hard work. While a sophomore in college she began what would become more than a nineteen year ordeal of medical interventions that would have stopped most people in their tracks. Despite several surgeries and nearly a year of chemotherapy as well as serious infections she graduated from college on time. Following her undergraduate work she went on to earn three graduate degrees, including a Ph.D. in communications, and several awards for the quality of her writing. Her capacity for hard work as well as her ability to generate outstanding publications and become a tenured professor has been an example of what a person can achieve when she or he is committed to their goals. Despite continuing suffering she remains a compassionate, gentle person.

Our Younger Son:

Our younger son was resistant to the idea of being in church but I didn't give him any choice. So, he presented me with a situation in which I had little or no choice. When he was ten or eleven years old, and it was time for the sermon, he would lay down in the first or second pew and go to sleep or at least pretend that he was doing so. My choices were simple. Either I would make an issue of it and upset him and probably the whole congregation or I would let it go. I chose to let it go. It was a lesson ably taught by our younger son!

He apparently wasn't all that much more pleased with his teachers than he was with me. He qualified to be in a program for the gifted and talented offered in the public schools of our town. However, even though I was teaching in that program, he wasn't allowed to join that program because he wouldn't do enough of the regular work that he was assigned to do. He was bored but the people who made the decisions decided that he needed to do the work that bored him before he could do anything that might challenge him. I realized from his experience how unresponsive the public school system can sometimes be to children who don't fit the mold. I also realized that I was quite limited in what I could do to help.

Fortunately for him and for us as parents we moved to a town in Vermont where there were people he could respect and work hard for. One was the drama teacher and the other was the music teacher. I was amazed at how much they helped him to develop his creative abilities. I am truly grateful for what they helped him to become.

When this same son got to college he worked hard as he studied theater. He continues to work long hours in doing lighting and sound design for theaters. He has also been amazingly creative in musical theater. He has written or co-written a number of musicals which have been produced in various places including off-Broadway in New York City.

Our younger son has also been a wonderful father to our younger granddaughter (Miette) and, with his wife, Diane, they have created a loving home for her. I am amazed at how much better a father he is than I was.

Our Grandchildren:

Zachory, Jamie and Miette have each given me a gift that I had not experienced in several years. It was the gift of allowing me to be a playful presence in their lives when they were quite young. They allowed me to devise imaginary characters and otherwise create situations in which I could be an elder who playfully participated in their world. I never had that experience as a child and I am truly grateful for being able to play with our grandchildren.

One of My Nephews:

Between our two families of origin Jane and I have several nieces and nephews as well several grandnieces and grandnephews. Most of them have endured difficult circumstances of one sort or another. However, there is one nephew whose life has spoken volumes about the suffering that human beings can endure. I will respect his privacy and not reveal his suffering except to say that it was painful emotionally and physically for him and even for those of us who watched and were limited in what we could do to help him. What is so remarkable about this nephew is that he found faith in God and has been actively involved in church for the majority of his life. In his case it is fair to say that church saved him from a meaningless and possibly self-destructive existence. Despite a painful chronic illness he makes a difference in a number of lives. I am grateful that he has found God in his life and has shared some of his spiritual journey with me and Jane.

CHAPTER 2
—FRIENDS

It is hard to overestimate the importance of friends. I have been blessed with a number of friends who have added to my life immensely. At almost every stage of my life, beginning with high school, they have appeared when I needed them.

High School and Early Working Years:

My memories of early childhood are dim and I do not recall being close to anyone in particular. However, by the time I was in high school I had a close friend whose name was David. He was the one who unknowingly introduced me to the Episcopal Church by inviting me to join the Boy Scouts. It was during my brief time with the Boy Scouts that I sneaked upstairs (we met in the basement of his church) to see what an Episcopal sanctuary looked like. That may not seem very exciting to you. However, those were the days of pre-Vatican Council II (about 1957) and Catholics were forbidden to even enter a Protestant Church. I'm not sure that David ever knew about my adventure of peering into the sanctuary where he worshipped but it was definitely an exciting event for me. Besides our time in school we spent time together fishing and talking about what teenaged boys talk about. He was a kind person who made room for me in his life.

I don't recall ever talking to him about what our futures might be like. However, many years later I discovered that we were both ordained clergy and both hospital chaplains. He stayed with the Episcopal Church and I became a United Methodist pastor and chaplain.

I did not find anyone who was as close a friend for about two years. This was, in part, because our family moved back to Leominster, Massachusetts at the end of my sophomore year. I had been out of touch with these students for nearly three years. One year later, at the end of my junior year, I quit school for a year to work because my family needed financial help. When I returned to high school I met Brian. We became close and I travelled with Brian and some other friends to track and speed-skating competitions throughout the Northeast. Brian was a competitor in both sports and he introduced me to a lot of people I otherwise would not have met. When we graduated from high school he went off to college and I went back to work for two years. We have stayed in touch over the years and still visit with each other. Brian was and still is a good friend. He accepted me just as I was, with all my shortcomings, and he valued me. He never made fun of me and, given my problem with stuttering, it would have been easy to do.

Another friend was a young Catholic seminarian named Peter. I don't remember his last name but I certainly do remember his kindness to me. He was studying for the Catholic priesthood in Jaffrey, New Hampshire at the Queen of Peace Mission Seminary. He accompanied the priest who came down from Jaffrey to the church I attended in Leominster (St. Leo's). As our friendship grew he invited me to visit the seminary in Jaffrey to meet other men who were studying for the priesthood. I gradually developed a sense that I was called to become a priest in this order.

While visiting Peter one weekend I learned a lesson in cultural sensitivity. He must have said something about being from Ireland and having a brogue. I immediately said that I didn't have any difficulty understanding him. He fired right back that he didn't have any difficulty understanding me either! I learned that I had just as much of an accent to his ears as he did to mine. I have since been more respectful of people's accents.

I made plans to enter the order that Peter was in as soon as possible in 1962. However, my father asked me not to go at that time. My father never asked me for anything except to work for a year to help our family. He usually told me what to do. Looking back he must have known that he wasn't going to live much longer. So I agreed to wait.

While I was waiting I worked in the laboratory at Solar Chemical Company in Leominster. I worked with two chemists and one other technician. The other technician was an older man from Czechoslovakia. Julius had been a member of a wealthy family and he was also a rabbinical student in his home country. His family had lost everything when the Nazis took over his country in 1938 and he had lost his career as a rabbi.

I learned two lessons from Julius that have been important to me. The first resulted from something that I did that hurt him. I asked the chemists if I could supervise the laboratory that Julius and I worked in. I was about twenty years old and thought that because I had had a college level course in chemistry as well as one in algebra that I knew more about the laboratory than Julius did. Perhaps I did but there was nothing to be gained, except for my pride, by putting Julius under my direction. When he discovered what I had done he told me that he would only work for a "graduate chemist." He had lost enough and he wasn't going to lose anymore if he could avoid it. I was immediately ashamed of myself and never did anything like that again.

As far as I knew Julius held no hard feelings. In fact, he taught me a helpful lesson. One day the two chemists met with Julius and me and suggested that each week we take turns bringing a topic, perhaps about a book or an article that we had read, and discuss it with the group as a continuing education experience. When Julius' turn came he told us the story of his losses and of having to leave Czechoslovakia twenty-three years earlier. He added, "But they can never take away what you know!" I gained a new appreciation for the value of knowledge for its own sake. I also gained a sense of empowerment by knowing that even if I lost all of my material possessions that I would still have my knowledge.

Catholic Seminary (College Level):

When I finally got to the undergraduate seminary that the order in Jaffrey, N.H. had in Winona, Minnesota (Brian drove me out there) I met a number of young men who shared my vocational goal. One of them was Tom. He was obviously struggling with his call to the priesthood because he had had a girlfriend the summer before entering the seminary. Worse yet, he sneaked out of the seminary dormitory one night to see this young woman and he was caught returning late to the dormitory by the man we knew as 'Father Superior." We never heard exactly what happened to Tom but we knew that he had committed a serious infraction of the rules.

I, too, was struggling with my call to the priesthood but not so much because of girls. I had an authority problem—a big authority problem. The Roman Catholic Church in 1963 was not the place to have an authority problem. I had the problem because of my relationship with my father—the retired U. S. Army Master Sergeant.

Actually, it wasn't simply authority that I found frustrating. It was the unreasonable use of authority that annoyed me. For example, I got into trouble one day when I asked a friend (George) to let me know how a fellow seminarian (John) was doing after he had had a chance to visit John in the infirmary. I was in Father Superior's office when I made this request of George. Father Superior immediately countermanded what I meant as a request by saying, "George, you don't have to tell Larry a thing!"

It also annoyed me that even though we were all attending classes across the street at St. Mary's College we couldn't stop in at the student union building to have a soft drink or visit with other college students. We were not a cloistered order and this rule made no sense to me.

Another lesson that I had a great deal of difficulty accepting was Father Superior's personal view of authority. Not only was it never to be questioned. There was also the message that he gave us one day that we "must do what our superior says even if he is a fool." That, he explained, was known as "riding to heaven on your superior's coat tails" and he wasn't joking! I have difficulty being grateful for this lesson but, on the other hand, it did help me to make my decision about leaving the Catholic seminary sooner rather than later.

Apparently, my friends in the seminary did not share my concerns since I seemed to be the only one complaining. After four months of not being able to find anyone who would listen empathically to my struggles with authority I left the seminary and finished the semester across the street in one of the college's regular dormitories. Then I transferred back to the state college in Fitchburg, Massachusetts.

College:

One of the young women that I met when I finally got to Fitchburg State College was a very special friend. Her name was Bernadette and I was attracted to her. She was a good and kind person. We dated a couple of times but her real gift to me was in something that she said about me. Commenting upon my personality she said to me and to several of our friends, "Larry is like a grape—a tough skin on the outside and all soft and squishy on the inside." She said it so kindly that I was able to hear it and realize that it might be time to do something about that tough skin.

Another young woman that I met when I was in college was named Barbara. She and I were in math classes together. She asked me to go to her sorority's prom and that night I discovered that she had very strong feelings for me. It was a revelatory experience for me—that a young woman could actually fall in love with me. We dated for awhile but then I learned another painful lesson about authority. She was a member of a very conservative Lutheran denomination and I was a Roman Catholic. When her pastor discovered that she was dating a Catholic he told her that she could not marry me. It was a crushing blow for both of us. I was used to an authoritarian church but I never dreamed I would encounter another one with the authority to forbid a marriage without any discussion. It was difficult because we still saw each other in class and around the campus but we gradually got over our grief.

Perhaps the friend who did the most to change the direction of my life was Al. He and I were fraternity brothers in Alpha Phi Omega—a national service fraternity. Al was also one of the people who organized an ecumenical discussion group for college students at Fitchburg State College in late 1965.

Al invited me to attend the opening session of this group. I agreed to attend. However, as the day drew nearer I began to have second thoughts. I couldn't see any reason to go and, on the morning of the day that the group was due to start, I told Al that I wouldn't be there that evening. However, Al didn't take "No" for an answer. He pleaded with me to go and, because he was a friend and a fraternity brother, I agreed to attend.

That night, November 1, 1965, was a turning point in my life. I saw Jane for the first time and I knew that she was someone special. We began to date several months later. Our relationship deepened and we were married almost fifteen months after we met. If Al had not persisted in his efforts to get me to attend the ecumenical group it is quite likely that I would have never met Jane. We were at the same college but she was a nursing student and I was a physics major. She was a Methodist and I was a Roman Catholic. She was in an army reserve nursing program and I was working part-time in a chemical laboratory. I expressed my gratitude to Al several years later when I wrote an article about this experience for the Fitchburg State College Alumni Magazine.

Working as a Chemist:

After my fourth change in major I finally graduated from college with a major in chemistry. I worked for Foster Grant for a total of four years and during that time I met a man named Bob who was to become a friend. He was a salesman for Coulter Electronics (manufacturers of instruments that measured small particles including blood cells) and he told me about a job opening at Polaroid Corporation in 1971. It took awhile but I finally found the right door to knock on. I was hired on July 1, 1971. Bob's guidance helped to turn my life in yet another direction as I began a deeper immersion in the world of optical and electron microscopes that would extend to January 31, 1979 at Polaroid.

One of my other friends during these days spent working as a scientist at Polaroid Corporation in the 1970s was a man named Jack. We worked in the same laboratory. He was the supervisor of the technicians and I was a scientist whose duties including developing analytical methods and applying them to product (photographic film ingredients) development issues. Jack had a great sense of humor and he helped me to laugh. He would see me in the corridor and call out to me, "Ain't it Awful! In my office in five minutes." It helps to know that the term "Ain't it Awful" was developed by a psychiatrist named Eric Berne and used by him to describe one of a variety of ways of spending time together that he termed "Games." Games, according to Berne, were unconsciously driven ways of communicating with the twin goals of avoiding intimacy and making certain that both parties felt badly after the transaction was over. Jack and I would spend time complaining about the various inefficiencies and apparent injustices in our department. It was both fun and depressing.

Jack also helped me to see, as Bernadette had so kindly done in college, that maybe it was time for me to improve my ways of dealing with people. He told me that when he first met me that he thought that I was "the troll from under the bridge." Jack was right. My people skills needed refining to say the least.

Local Churches in Massachusetts:

There were many other fine people I met at work but it was in our local church in Waltham, Massachusetts that I met a man who made a profound impact on my thinking. His name was Sam. Sam was from the island nation of Sri Lanka (formerly Ceylon) and he was in Massachusetts to complete the coursework for his Ph.D. To support himself he worked as an associate pastor at the Congregational church that our family attended.

We became good friends over the period of a year. During the course of that year I sought out Sam to talk about a problem that I was having. I had enrolled at Andover Newton Theological Seminary to test out my sense of call again. I only took one course because I wasn't ready to leave my job as a scientist. It was a course on urban ministry. I took it because I was living in an urban area and wanted to know more about ministry in this setting. However, I was deeply disappointed with the way the course was structured.

It helps to know that in the 1970s there was a great deal of stress in a lot of cities in America that was caused by the federally-mandated busing of students to racially integrate the public schools. In Boston the chairperson of the Boston School Committee was well-known for her dealings with the school committee. For whatever reason, the professor thought it worthwhile to devote well over half of the class time to the latest activities of the Boston School Committee and its chairperson. I was so frustrated that I quit the course halfway through the semester.

Then I felt guilty—really guilty—because I had once again, like back in 1963, left a seminary and turned away from what I thought was God's call to ministry. I sought out Sam to talk over my feelings. Sam listened to my story and then he responded with a message that I have never forgotten. He said, "Larry, you might do more good as a lay person in the Church than you ever would as a clergy person."

What a radical and liberating thought! I had always looked up to the clergy as somehow more important in the life of the Church than any lay person could ever hope to be. It freed me to think about what I could do with my life. I have since used this story with a number of people who have talked to me about ministry.

I had another friend in this same church. Ray taught anatomy and physiology at a college in Boston. So we had a shared interest in science. We also served as deacons in the church. One day he shared with me that he had had a calling to ministry following his return from World War II. He admitted to me that he had turned away from that calling to earn his Ph.D. Ray seemed sad when he shared that story with me and, once again, I wondered if I was turning away from my calling.

At about the same time that I was having these conversations with Sam and Ray I was also watching helplessly as another scenario unfolded in our local congregation. The senior pastor, Ken, had been warmly received when he arrived at the church. My wife Jane and I became friends with Ken and his wife Sharman. However, it wasn't too long before a small group of people in the church began to criticize Ken because of his leadership style.

We watched as the pressure grew to get rid of him. Fortunately, Ken was able to find another church before he could be fired. However, in the process of watching my friend and his wife undergo this transition I saw a dark side of the local church that I did not like. At a meeting of the board of deacons not long before Ken resigned a fellow deacon turned to explain what was happening as I expressed frustration with the way the congregation was treating Ken. He said, "Larry, it's just like down at the office. When you have a problem (with staff) you do what you have to do to take care of it." I didn't know what to say but I knew that I had just heard an important message about the way that some people in the local church think.

There didn't appear to be anywhere in the process for prayer or otherwise discerning God's will for Ken and the congregation. I was all the more disappointed because this was another example of authority being used in what seemed an unreasonable way.

We left that congregation because of our disappointment over the way that the pastor was treated. Another friend offered a new direction in church life for us. I had shared the story of my disappointment with the church and Tom offered the ultimate in low key approaches to evangelism. He simply said, "You might like the church that I attend." In fact, we did attend worship and otherwise get involved at the church where Tom and his wife Shay were members. It was more theologically conservative than we were used to but it seemed like the right place to be.

Among many other interactions that we had at that church was the experience I had teaching an adult Sunday School class. There were about a dozen adults in the class and one of them, Bob, had approached me with the request that I teach them "how to live as a Christian." He also said, "Don't try to tell us what the Bible says. We've been studying the Bible for thirty years. We know what it says. We want to know how to apply it."

Indeed, they did know the Bible much better than I did. However, we had much to learn from each other. I respected their knowledge and worked to draw out of them what most of them already knew about living as a Christian. The class went well.

As part of our sharing in this class I talked about my sense that I was called into pastoral ministry. They suggested that we pray about my calling as a group until we came to a consensus about my call. After about a year, it became clear to all of us that I was being called into pastoral ministry. Though I have forgotten many of their names

I will never forget how much support the members of that adult Sunday School class gave to me and to Jane as we prepared to go to seminary.

Before I got there, however, I had another spiritual obstacle to overcome. While the class members were praying for us I felt like I was in turmoil emotionally and spiritually. I was caught up in an inner struggle with something that I couldn't name and that I didn't understand. I brought all of these vague feelings to Tom, the man who invited us to come to the church that he attended. He listened and said something that I instantly recognized as true. He said, "You know, there's such a thing as spiritual warfare." Saint Paul described the reality of spiritual forces contending with us in Ephesians 6:10-17. Tom helped me to reframe what I was undergoing and thereby helped me to seek God's help in coping with the struggle. In other words, he helped me to recognize that there were spiritual forces at work that did not want me to pursue my call to ministry.

Tom also did something else for me while we were working at Polaroid. He invited me to attend a Bible study group that was meeting on Wednesdays at noon in another engineer's office. It was a study on St. Paul's letter to the Romans and it lasted six months. At the end of each session we took time for prayer. However, the time for praying got so long that we had to create a separate group for prayer that met on Thursdays. By the time that I left Polaroid to head to Maine there were about twenty of us meeting on Wednesdays for Bible study and eight or nine of us gathering for prayer on Thursdays. It demonstrated to me what God could do with a very small group of people who were committed to study and prayer—even at work.

Before I left Massachusetts for the seminary in Maine something else happened that moved me a little further along the path of deeper self-awareness. It was a lesson that humbled me in a way that I needed to be humbled. One day around 1978, while I was working at Polaroid Corporation, I walked by our department secretary's office as she was pouring out her heart to my boss, Bob. She was voicing her frustration at dealing with a department made up mostly of men. She was young and very pretty and the men would tease her and apparently make her feel bad. I walked by just as she said, "Now, you take Larry for example. No one ever gets the upper hand on him!"

I stopped in my tracks. I was struck by what Rosemary had just said. I had never fully realized, although others had tried to tell me, how quick I was to respond to someone else's attempts to put me down. I would have admitted to being willing to stand up for myself but I never realized that I had to win in every exchange. Overhearing Rosemary's comment didn't solve my problem but it reminded me once again that I had some work to do on who I was—especially since I always had to be right!

Seminary:

When I finally got to Bangor Theological Seminary (Bangor, Maine) I stayed to complete the Master of Divinity degree. The support of family, friends, professors and, later, parishioners all were instrumental in enabling me to complete not only the study but also the other tasks required for ordination.

One of the first experiences I had upon arriving at the seminary was a chance meeting with a student beginning his senior year named

Michael. He told me something that I didn't expect to hear. He said, "If you think that you left the 'world' behind you when you came to seminary, think again." It was a disillusioning experience because I had, at least unconsciously, expected that the seminary would be a different kind of place than what I had been used to in industry, school and even some of the local churches we had joined.

It's not that the seminary campus was a place of extraordinary sins. Not at all. It was a place of ordinary human behaviors that sometimes took the focus off of why I thought we were there. I expected to join a community of people dedicated to growth as spiritual persons. There was some effort in that area but most of what went on at the seminary was academic. The faculty appeared to be mostly concerned with having us master ideas and information which, admittedly, were important to functioning as ministers. It's just that I was looking for more emphasis on spiritual community.

One of the people who reminded me of how the world was very much alive in the seminary was a bright young man named Bob. Bob had been an assistant coach at a small college. He knew that I had been a senior engineer with an electronics company just before entering seminary. He said to me one day, "I don't understand you. At least when I finish seminary I can expect to make more money than I did as a coach. You'll never make as much money as you did!" I had no good answer to his assertion. I had not gone to the seminary expecting to make more money some day. I had gone because God had called me.

However, another student at the same seminary, Mel, was an absolute inspiration to me. I thought that I was unusual in taking the step of going to seminary at the age of thirty-seven. There were, in fact, many students in my age group and several who were older.

Mel was much older. He was sixty-seven when he decided to attend seminary. I had moved from the Boston area. He had moved from Cincinnati, Ohio. I had left behind a career but Mel had retired after a long career and he felt God leading him to seminary. I was amazed at his willingness to undertake the demands of seminary at an age when most people think they have done enough. Meeting Mel was definitely a high point in my seminary experience.

While at Bangor Theological Seminary I made many other friends. Among the most important of my friends were a group of three United Methodist men: Terry, Steve and George. The four of us were known on campus as "The Methodist Mafia." We were all fairly large men and we all carried the same kind of leather briefcases. We were in most of the same classes. So I suppose that we stood out when we were together.

I found their friendship on and off campus to be very important. They were especially supportive to me in 1984 when it seemed that I was facing heart problems. It is one of the advantages of the United Methodist Church that we are a connectional system. Not only are the local churches connected in an annual conference system. The pastors are members of the annual conference as well. I knew that I could rely on Terry, Steve and George, among many others, if I needed help.

Among those pastors whom I knew that I could count on were a clergy couple whose names were Lloyd and Sally. At the time that I met them Lloyd was a pastor and Sally was a student like me. Lloyd helped me to get appointed to a student parish by speaking to the District Superintendent (a supervisor of pastors in the United Methodist Church). Then, once I had been appointed to the parish he and Sally offered to let me stay at their home near the seminary during the week so that I wouldn't have to commute ninety miles from the parsonage to the seminary every day. I returned home to our family and the parish on weekends. We did this for an academic year. I don't know how I would have made it through seminary that year without the generosity of Lloyd and Sally and the patience of my family.

Church Pastorates:

When I completed my seminary training I was appointed to my first full-time parish in north central Maine. There I met a man who became a close friend. Jim was a social worker and a part-time pastor in a little town about twenty miles away. We met for coffee once a month and exchanged stories and ideas. He was the one who helped me to understand one of the fundamental dynamics of how human beings treat one another. He drew a circle on a napkin and wrote the word "us" inside the circle and the word "them" outside of the circle. "The world," he said, "is divided into two groups—us and them." Obviously, this simple paradigm doesn't explain all of the intricacies of human behavior. However, it does help to make sense of how we end up in conflicts.

Jim also helped me to synthesize my ideas about trust into a paper that we co-authored in 1989 in the Journal of Religion and Health. Basically, my idea was that there are three levels of human encounter and thus three levels of trust. Jim's contribution to the paper was to suggest that those three levels of trust can be destroyed by what he described as a "world-shattering event." He meant that there are situations that arise between family members, friends or colleagues that can be so damaging to the relationship that they shatter our ability and even our desire to find meaning and hope in the relationship. This insight helped me to make sense of situations in my life in which trust had either been threatened or actually destroyed.

Molly was an Episcopal priest that I met in my second full-time parish—i.e. in Swanton, Vermont.. She was an unusual person in that she had never attended seminary yet had been ordained as a priest. She did this by studying for the qualifying exams for ordination at home. I have never met anyone else who was able to be that disciplined in their studies.

Molly stands out in my memory for another reason. I had asked her to write a letter of recommendation for me as part of the application process for a doctor of ministry program at Boston University. Like three other people before her (Bernadette in college and Jack and Rosemary at Polaroid Corporation) she reminded me that I still needed to improve my people skills. She noted in her letter of recommendation that I didn't "suffer fools gladly." Indeed, I didn't and I needed to be told so.

Romeo was another friend whom I met in Swanton. He was a Catholic priest and an associate pastor in the local Catholic Church. He was also an avid genealogist. He would travel to Montreal, Quebec on the bus to pour over birth and death records to try to document family connections. He did all this while he was legally blind. He never complained about his limitations. He modeled patience and acceptance of one's situation.

Veterans Administration Chaplaincy:

Richard and Lillian are friends whom we met in 1989 following an ecumenical worship service not too far from where I was serving as a chaplain at the Veterans Administration (VA) hospital in Vermont. Richard also worked at the VA hospital as a nurse. We are still friends even though Jane and I moved from Vermont to Maine and then to California. Richard was our daughter's and son-in-law's wedding photographer. Richard and I met once a month for several years for breakfast and a discussion of the latest struggles within the VA healthcare system. We also shared something of our spiritual journeys. It was good to have someone who understood the VA, was a Christian and was able to maintain a confidence.

During my first two years at the VA hospital I completed three units of what are known as Clinical Pastoral Education (CPE). They are designed to give local clergy, as well as those preparing for chaplaincy, the opportunity for supervised clinical training in pastoral care usually in a hospital setting. As part of the training there are a number of group meetings designed to allow CPE students to review and reflect upon what happened as they visited patients. This is a very useful tool for discovering why we do what we do and what kind of feelings that we are experiencing during our pastoral visits.

During one of these sessions I was confronted by one of the other CPE students. I have long since forgotten what issue he raised for me but it must have touched on something very upsetting for me, probably an unconscious issue, because I was soon weeping as I tried to respond to what was being said to me. The supervisor did not intervene presumably because he did not see anything inappropriate happening. When he finally called for a break I was still quite upset.

That was when a remarkable thing happened. A friend in the group got up and walked outside with me and talked to me in comforting ways about what had just happened. His name was Al. It was very kind of him to take the time to share my anguish. However, it was especially remarkable because Al walked with me despite the fact that he normally moved from one place to another using a motorized wheelchair. Al had multiple sclerosis. He walked with me using Canadian crutches and a great deal of physical strength. He was a well-built but large man. He had to partially shuffle and partially drag his lower body as he maneuvered to walk. I don't know anyone who ever made such an extraordinary physical effort to help me. In later years Al, who was a veteran, would visit me at the VA hospital whenever he came in for a checkup.

Jim was another friend while I was at the VA hospital. He was a physician and a very well-known ethicist. We worked together on the hospital ethics committee. Several times we interviewed patients about whom someone had raised a question concerning the ethical dimension of that person's care. He was generous with his time and knowledge and always listened carefully both to what the patient, the staff and his/her family and I had to say. I gained a great deal of clinical experience with him as we worked together in a consultative role for the ethics committee. When Jim left the VA hospital to join the staff of a nearby major medical center he invited me to join the ethics committee that he chaired at the medical center and I asked him to fill the same type of position on the VA ethics committee that I now chaired.

By the end of 1991, a few years before Jim left the VA, I was appointed to be the chief of the chaplaincy service. It was a wonderful, challenging and fulfilling position. However, I soon realized that I needed some kind of support group to be able to cope with the emotional and spiritual demands of the job. Two clergy colleagues filled that role for me for several years. Dale and Bob were both Baptist ministers. Dale pastored a local congregation and Bob, although a part-time pastor for several years, really was interested in Biblical scholarship, seminary teaching and, eventually, editing and translating books that seminary students and other scholars would use.

I never discussed individual patient's issues with them. However, I did share my struggles with the VA hospital's financial, organizational and political problems. I also spoke about my efforts to provide a variety of pastoral care interventions in the lives of a group of very special and often misunderstood people—the veterans and their families.

Bob and Dale would likewise share the struggles they had to cope with in either the local parish or the seminary. Thanks to Bob's encouragement and support I was invited to teach two courses for Bangor Theological Seminary at their then Hanover, N.H. campus. Bob was also the coordinator for a day-long professional education program held every year by the Vermont-New Hampshire Conference of the American Baptist Church. He invited me to be the presenter and worship leader at the conference in the late 1990s. I was delighted to accept.

Both Bob and Dale also invited me to come into their local parishes and lead a training program for a parish visitation program. They were very open to my presence in their parishes—a trait not always found amongst clergy. Dale was also helpful to me professionally by being willing to be available for emergencies at the VA hospital and to lead worship in the hospital chapel on Sundays periodically so that I could have some time off.

Another good friend while I was at the VA hospital was named Andy. He was a psychiatrist who had been a family physician. We worked together in a number of ways. We were on the ethics committee and we did several consults on ethical issues in patient care together. When

I finally got my Doctor of Ministry degree in 1995 Andy helped me to secure an appointment as an instructor in the Dartmouth Medical School Department of Psychiatry. This made it possible for me to teach psychiatry residents about spirituality. We also worked together, sometimes on a daily basis, in dealing with the needs of psychiatric patients. With his support I led three groups each week that focused on spirituality. One group was with the patients on the inpatient psychiatric unit. Two groups were with the outpatient program for veterans with Post Traumatic Stress Disorder.

Andy and I would also attend the patients' coffee hour twice a week on the inpatient psychiatric unit. We did this because we enjoyed the coffee and cookies but we were really there to be accessible to the patients. The veterans were able to talk to us in a more open, less formal setting than in our offices or in groups. A great many mental health and spiritual, including Biblical, issues were raised and discussed in those coffee hours.

Crisis at the VA

In November 2001 I reached a turning point in my career with the VA hospital. I was assaulted for the fourth time at the VA. This time it was by a physician. The assault did not cause any physical damage. It was meant playfully but it was a truly unfortunate experience because I reacted violently. I didn't cause any physical harm but I came very close to doing so. It took me two days to summon the courage to confront this physician with my feelings of anger over what he did to me. The experience was shattering to me not so much because of what had actually happened but because of what could have happened. I reacted without thinking and I could not live with myself for having reacted so violently. I felt as if this event had destroyed my career at the VA and it had.

One of my supporters was another psychiatrist who had been supervising my counseling cases. Gail was able to see the harm that occurred to me because of this assault and she strongly recommended that I go on medical leave until the matter could be resolved. I did, in fact, go on medical leave and I applied for disability for Post Traumatic Stress Disorder after being seen several times by a psychiatrist in private practice. The disability pension was granted and I left the VA.

Post VA Hospital:

My wife and I moved to the coast of Maine in part to get away from the negative associations that I had as a result of my VA experience and in part to live near the ocean. While in Maine I developed a network of clergy friends and I led worship as what is known as a supply pastor (one who fills in for a pastor who is away or unavailable) in what developed into a network of eleven local churches.

Among my clergy friends was a pastor named Arlin. I was a supply pastor for him several times and our wives got to know each other as well. The four of us built a close friendship as we found in one another kindred spirits. We shared not only our ideas about faith but also our experiences of growing in our faith. We became as close as any couple that we have known over the last forty years.

Along with being a supply pastor I also worked as a part-time coordinator of pastoral care for a local health care system (one day per week) and as a hospice chaplain for the home health nurses in that health care system (also one day per week). While there I became friends with the clergy group who volunteered to be on call for pastoral emergencies at the local hospital. One of them, an Episcopal priest named Ralph, recruited me to lead a training program known as Alternative Clinical Pastoral Education.

This program, which was similar to the CPE programs that I had completed, was designed to provide clinical training and supervision for people who were preparing for the permanent diaconate in the Episcopal diocese of Maine as well as for people who needed the training to become pastors. Three people enrolled in the program and we worked together for over six months. Rob, Isabel and Kate trusted me to guide them in their clinical training and I appreciated their trust. All three were ordained at the end of the program—i.e. this was the final element in their training.

Mac and Doris were among our other friends on the coast of Maine. We met them in a local United Methodist church. Although they were several years older than we were we found them to be caring people who shared our interests in the Church. Among other activities we shared an interest in French food and we would go out to dinner at a nearby French restaurant.

When we left Maine to move to California it felt like I was leaving my support group behind. I wondered where we would find new friends. I need not have worried. We now live in San Jose, California and have been blessed by a number of new friendships.

Not only are we involved in the Campbell United Methodist Church and St. Mark's Episcopal Church. Both of us are also involved in several church or church-related groups as well. We have friends at both churches as well as in the mobile home park where we live. Our daughter and son-in-law live just two miles away. God continues to be good to us.

CHAPTER 3
—MENTORS

I have spent much of my life looking for mentors. However, I was also wary of anyone who would have too much authority over me. How much was too much authority? It's hard to describe except to say that it was whatever reminded me of my father—a man who never told me that he loved me and who abused his authority over me. Yet, I did find mentors—many of them. Some of them helped me for many years while others intervened only briefly.

HIGH SCHOOL MENTORS:

My earliest mentors were coaches in the public school system in Lunenburg, Massachusetts. Richard and Floyd each asked me to manage athletic teams. Richard offered me the position of manager of the junior varsity basketball team. Floyd later asked me if I would be the co-manager of the varsity basketball, baseball and track teams. I welcomed each of these positions because they were opportunities to be accepted for something more than being smart. Richard and Floyd were kind and respectful towards me. They showed me how to lead without being violent. They showed me the importance of team play.

The vice-principal of Leominster High School was a mentor to me just briefly. In 1961 he was a major help to me in beginning a career that lasted over eighteen years. I didn't know John very well but when I needed his help he literally said the right thing at the right time. I had quit school after my junior year in order to work to help my family. Then I returned to finish high school. It was May of my senior year and I knew that there was no chance to go to college at that point. I had very little money and my family had none. I knew that I had to go back to work but I had no idea how to get a more interesting job than the ones that I had held.

One day I asked John for his advice. He heard me out and then noted that I had done well in science and mathematics. He asked if I had ever considered working in a laboratory as a technician. I hadn't. However, within the month I had secured a part-time job as a laboratory technician for a plastics manufacturer known as Solar Chemical Corporation. When I graduated in June I immediately started working full-time at their laboratory and continued there until I went to college over two years later. This beginning step led to my eighteen-year involvement in chemistry and physics laboratories.

A SPIRITUAL MENTOR:

I had other kinds of mentors. One was Father Robert. He was a Roman Catholic priest who officiated at our marriage at St. Bernard's Catholic Church in Fitchburg, Massachusetts. He made an impact on me for three reasons. First, he was the only person who believed in Jane and me enough to officiate at our marriage. He worked hard to help us get ready for marriage. He took care of a lot of paperwork that was required by the Roman Catholic Church in those days because Jane was not a Roman Catholic.

Second, Father Robert also criticized me for the way that I was living my Christian life and rightfully so. One day, after confessing my sins to Father Robert he got angry with me and said, "Larry, you're nothing but an intellectual Christian." It was a stunning criticism and one that was another in a long line of reminders that I needed to change my life. What he meant was that my actions were all-too-often not consistent with my beliefs.

The third way that Father Robert made an impact on me was to teach me what he referred to as the principle of "Epikaya." I'm not positive about the spelling but the word comes from the Greek text of one of St. Paul's letters in the Bible—the book of Colossians. Father Robert explained that it referred to a little-known teaching in the Roman Catholic Church. The teaching was that a person had to follow the leading of God's Holy Spirit even if doing so meant that the person was in conflict with Roman Catholic Church law. That was tremendously liberating to me.

SCIENTIFIC MENTORS:

In 1964 I was hired by a chemist named Michael to work as his laboratory technician to make very specialized chemicals known as organo-metallic compounds. I worked for Mike for two and one half years and he taught me an enormous amount about making chemicals as well as about working hard. It was not unusual in his laboratory for me to have five operations going on at the same time—two or three chemical reactions, a distillation, a crystallization and filtration and to be cleaning up glassware or running a boiling point test. Mike was a stickler for detail and for good reason. There literally was a right way to do everything and if I did not do it the right way I risked ruining the product or even setting the laboratory on fire. In that way Mike was like my father and I sometimes reacted to him as if he was my father. Nevertheless, I only left his employ because his company was going under financially.

During my first professional job at Foster Grant, Inc. I met a man from Belgium who became a different kind of mentor. His name was Pierre and he became a friend as well as a mentor. Pierre directed a laboratory that focused on polymer (plastics) physics. For whatever reason, he decided to help me with my career. He suggested several studies that we did together. On at least a few occasions he even insisted that I put my name first on the report. That was a remarkable gesture on his part considering that I was clearly the junior person both in knowledge and experience. He taught me that one doesn't have to be first. He also taught me the importance of helping others to develop their abilities.

Pierre was remarkable in at least one other way. Pierre had temper tantrums—big temper tantrums! When he was upset everyone within a radius of a hundred feet knew it. There were occasions when Pierre was so upset that he literally slammed the door to his laboratory so loudly that everyone on that floor could hear it.

Pierre taught me something important about anger. It wasn't that I should go around slamming doors when I was upset. It was, instead, that I should find ways to express my anger. I had grown up believing that it was both unsafe and sinful to be angry. The unsafe part came from my father's threats to react violently if I got angry and threatened him. The sinful part came from growing up in the Roman Catholic Church where I was taught that anger was a sin. Not only was it a sin. It was one of the so-called "Seven Deadly Sins." It took a lot of therapy, a master's degree in counseling and training in Clinical Pastoral Education before I began to heal from that anger.

When I moved from Foster Grant, Inc. to Polaroid Corporation in 1971 I discovered another mentor. His name was Bob and he was the senior supervisor of the laboratory where I worked. Bob introduced me to the world of electron microscopes and also the world of fine (very small) particle size analysis. To give the reader an idea of the scale that we were working at both in the electron microscopes and the fine particle size analyzers we routinely measured particles around one micrometer or less in diameter. A micrometer is one twenty-fifth of a mil and a mil is one-thousandth of an inch. So we were observing and measuring particles that were one twenty-five thousandth of an inch or less in size. He did not hover over me when he gave me an assignment. Instead, he trusted me to conduct investigations into a number of analytical and product development issues.

However, for reasons of industrial security I wasn't allowed to publish papers describing the analytical methods that I developed. There was only one occasion while at Polaroid Corporation that I was allowed to give an invited talk outside of the company. It was on the precision (reproducibility) of fine particle size analysis. The day before I was due to give that talk I was called into the divisional vice president's office. Peter told me, "Don't tell them anything." He meant that I should not reveal anything about the technology that Polaroid Corporation had developed or was working on. That felt a little like dealing with my father again because I had no choice but to comply.

There was another Peter, a senior scientist, who tried to teach me a lesson about discretion that I was reluctant to learn. It's a long technical argument but basically I was embroiled in a dispute with another Polaroid laboratory about the way to photograph very small particles through an optical microscope. To make my point I wrote a three page single-spaced memorandum citing all of the reasons, including my sources, why the other laboratory's procedures were wrong. Worse yet, I sent copies to a number of senior people in the division I was in. Peter (the senior scientist) was on the distribution list. He met me in the corridor and basically told me that I was right but that I had gone about dealing with the problem in a way that irritated several people. I knew he was right but I was still annoyed with the staff of the other laboratory for not admitting that their procedures were wrong. It was another signal that I needed to change my ways.

That same message was reinforced a year or two later by my department manager. Jack had no criticism of my technical work. In face, he supported me in being promoted twice. He did, however, one day refer to the "iron rod" that I had up my back. He was referring to my unwillingness to "bend" when I was right. It was another signal that I noticed but wasn't sure how to accommodate.

PASTORAL MENTORS:

The first mentor that I had in preparation for ministry was actually a family friend. Harry and his wife Eva had known Jane since she was twelve years old. When I met Jane I soon grew to like Harry and Eva. Harry became something of a father figure to me. He was a wise and gentle person who, with Eva, supported Jane and me during some difficult times.

Harry also opened my eyes to the denomination in which I am now an ordained minister. It happened when our family moved to Maine in 1979. We were looking for a church in which to worship during Holy

Week. Harry was the substitute pastor at the Saco United Methodist Church and, since we knew him, we went to worship several times during Holy Week of that year. In fact, I was so astounded by Harry's preaching that I said to him after the Easter Sunday service, "I'm amazed to hear a mainline pastor preaching Jesus Christ crucified and risen."

That was an amazingly brash thing for me to say to anyone let alone a family friend and senior pastor. It may help to know that I had just spent a year and a half in a very conservative church and, apparently, I had assimilated some of their prejudice against mainline churches. Harry was very gracious about it. We stayed in touch over the years and several years before he died I told Harry how pivotal he had been in helping me to decide to become a United Methodist minister.

The person who helped me to understand some more of what it meant to be a minister was the pastor of a church near the seminary in Bangor, Maine. Richard was literally a classmate of my mother but we didn't discover that for awhile. One of the exercises that he assigned to me was to go through the Bible and find every instance of someone being called by God into God's service.

I completed my assignment with some anxiety because I wasn't certain that I had found every example of God's call in the Bible. I arrived at the church prepared to discuss the examples that I had found. When I started to explain about my list Richard cut me off. He said, "Never mind about that. Which call is yours?" I thought for a moment and decided that the call of Samuel in 1 Samuel 3 was the Biblical narrative that most closely paralleled my experience.

Samuel, while still a boy, heard God call him on three separate occasions. Finally, Samuel's mentor, Eli, said to him "Go, lie down; and if he calls you, you shall say, 'Speak, Lord, for your servant is listening.'" (1

Samuel 3:9a NRSV) It took me two tries at seminaries and a master's degree in counseling before I got it right—i.e. before I heard what God was saying and obeyed. Like the boy Samuel I heard God calling but I was hindered from responding. It wasn't that I didn't understand or recognize God's voice. It was probably a combination of not being willing to submit to the demands (authority) of seminary life and finding counseling an intriguing substitute that would also help me to understand some of my own problems.

After that first year of seminary, Richard continued to be my mentor. I was assigned to a parish made up of three small United Methodist churches in what is known as the Down East portion of Maine's coast. Richard met with me and two or three other student pastors once a month to discuss our experiences of parish life. He challenged us to think about what was going on in the dynamics of parish life. For example, I brought a concern early on that the lay people weren't working with me very well for reasons that I did not understand. He asked me to think about who the person was in each local church that held the most power. I began to realize that there were people who because of longevity in the church, social standing in the town or force of personality had a lot more influence on what happened in the church than I did. As the pastor, I had clear lines of responsibility and authority in the church according to the rules laid out in The United Methodist Book of Discipline. However, I also had to take into account the way that the church people used their power. Richard helped me to learn this and other lessons.

As his time as a formal mentor for me was coming to an end, Richard helped me with another very difficult issue in ministry. I was ready to be ordained for the second time in The United Methodist Church. The first ordination was to the order of deacon and the second was to the order of elder. I had completed all of the requirements including an hour long interview with the bishop.

Everything had gone well until I began to think about the questions that all candidates for United Methodist ministry are asked just before the ordination ceremony. One of the questions was and is "Are you going on to perfection?" I was nearly overwhelmed with anxiety at the thought of trying to answer this question. I could not imagine saying "Yes" since I was painfully aware of how far away I was from perfection.

I went to Richard with my anxiety and asked what I should do. I really thought that perhaps I should not be ordained. He very calmly shared how he had coped with that question nearly forty years earlier. He explained that for him "going on to perfection" meant doing the best we can each day with the grace that we have been given that day. That made sense to me and I was ordained as an elder in The United Methodist Church in 1984.

After completing my time with Richard I was assigned to meet regularly with a new mentor. George was an experienced United Methodist pastor. He, too, gathered a small group of us for monthly meetings to discuss case studies that each of us brought. His guidance was instrumental in helping me to cope with the needs of the next parish to which I was assigned. The parish was full-time and it was made up of two churches located in north-central Maine. The larger of the two parishes had a self-image problem. For that matter, the entire town had a self-image problem due to the rather pungent odor caused by sulfur emissions from a local paper mill.

The church was not only affected by the smell of the town. It had gone through a terrible confrontation within its own walls over whether to build a new church. When the night of the parish vote came the congregation was split. The people in favor of the proposal to build a new church literally sat on one side of the sanctuary and those against the proposal sat on the other side. The vote was also split right down the middle. Following that tie vote a number of those who favored building the new church left that United Methodist church.

By the time that I was assigned to be their pastor the attitudes had hardened to the point where there seemed no way to bring the sides together. No one thought to tell me about this problem before or during the interview for the position of pastor. However, within a very short period of time it became clear that there were problems in this church.

One of the actions that I convinced the church to take was to hire a consultant. Doug had been a church consultant for several years and later a member of the faculty of a protestant seminary. The story of what he did for the local church that I served is interesting but it's his role as a mentor that I want to highlight.

During my program to earn a Doctor of Ministry degree I had to do two fieldwork assignments in addition to the coursework and the thesis. Doug supervised me in one of those fieldwork programs. It was a study of various methods of facilitating church financial stewardship. This went on for several months and then I wrote a summary report. Because he had consulted with the church I was serving he was able to see where I had downplayed the significance of local church history and politics. He urged me to redo my analysis and include a wider variety of factors to explain why this church was having difficulty raising enough money to support itself. Later, when I left for a parish in Northwestern Vermont this report formed the basis of a document that I wrote for the next pastor to describe the ways that this church functioned.

When I arrived in Vermont I found a new mentor. Stan had helped me years earlier when I was just beginning ministry. He taught the pastoral care segment of a two week program designed to prepare new pastors for the day-to-day aspects of church ministry. Later, when he was a District Superintendent in the Troy Annual Conference of The United Methodist Church he helped me to transfer from Maine to Vermont.

His leadership made a difference in my life in a number of ways. He encouraged me to complete the work for the Doctor of Ministry degree at Boston University. He supported me in dealing with the needs of a church that was even more dysfunctional than the one in north-central Maine. In particular, when a segment of the church membership decided to complain about me at the annual meeting of the church, known as the "Charge Conference," he refused to be swayed by their exaggerated negativity about me.

Stan was helpful in at least two other ways. When I mentioned that I had an interest in hospital chaplaincy he remembered that. Then, instead of being inhibited by the pastoral vacancy that my leaving the church would create, he told me of an opening for a part-time hospital chaplain at the Veterans Administration hospital in White River Junction, Vermont. I pursued the opportunity and it led eventually to a full-time position as the chief chaplain.

The other way that Stan made a difference was when our daughter was diagnosed with cancer. He was supportive of our family in a variety of ways. One way was truly remarkable. The day that our daughter was admitted to Massachusetts General Hospital for a biopsy of her leg Stan drove from Burlington, Vermont to Boston, Massachusetts just to be able to pray with Laura and me as we waited for her to be admitted. It was approximately a ten hour round trip for him just to have a few minutes with us at the hospital. I was amazed that anyone would do that for us.

WOMEN MENTORS:

Another person who mentored me was a woman professor named Carrie at a school of theology in Boston. I had completed all of the requirements for the Doctor of Ministry degree except for the thesis. Professor Carrie agreed to be my advisor and she had both the background and the temperament to work well with me. She helped me to develop the proposal for the thesis and then she shepherded me through the research and the writing up of the research. She guided me through the defense of the thesis and I was awarded the Doctor of Ministry degree in January of 1995.

Another woman who mentored me was Gail. She was a psychiatrist and a professor of psychiatry at a nearby medical school when I was the chief chaplain at the Veterans Affairs hospital in Vermont. She began to mentor me in the part of my work as a chaplain which I devoted to group and individual counseling. Gail met with me once a week for an hour to review what happened during my group and one-to-one counseling sessions during most of ten years. She also helped me to develop a number of my ideas about spirituality. She was the senior author of an article that we co-authored on the spirituality of Vietnam Veterans.

Cindy combined the roles of supervisor and mentor for me at the next healthcare system. When I left the Veterans Administration hospital and moved to Maine she hired me to be the coordinator of pastoral care at Northeast Healthcare on the coast of Maine. She supported all of my efforts both to do my assigned duties and to expand the position. She invited me to join the Ethics Committee and she supported me in becoming the hospice chaplain for the Visiting Nurse program that was part of Northeast Health. Cindy also affirmed my efforts to create a plan, in conjunction with our development office staff, to solicit funding from private donors to endow a permanent chaplaincy position at Northeast Health. This project succeeded in raising the money needed to establish a permanent chaplaincy program after I left this healthcare system.

I feel blessed to have found as many mentors as I did. Each of them had unique gifts and made a positive impact on my development as a person and in developing and using my skills in whatever position that I held.

CHAPTER 4
—TEACHERS OF ALL KINDS

EARLY TEACHERS OF RELIGION:

There is a saying attributed to an unknown Buddhist teacher. The teacher was reported to have said, "When the student is ready the teacher will appear." That has certainly been true in my life. I have been surrounded by teachers throughout most of my life—many of them outside academic circles. When I was ready to learn I benefited from the lessons offered to me.

One of the people whom I apparently wasn't sure that I wanted to learn from was the Catholic priest in Berlin, Germany who was teaching me the responses that I was to make as an acolyte at the Catholic mass. I learned the Latin responses and I eventually served as an acolyte for a number of years. However, there was one class session that I did not attend. I sat on the steps of the priest's office and I waited until the time for the lesson was over. Then I went home. My father heard about my absenteeism in short order and he asked me why I didn't go. I lied to him and told him that I had gone to the lesson. How I ever dared to lie is beyond me. Why he didn't punish me severely is also beyond my understanding.

However, I believe it was this same priest as well as a nun who taught me the lessons from <u>The Baltimore Catechism Number One</u> that I needed to know for my "First Holy Communion." I don't remember much from those lessons. However, I do remember the emphasis on the real presence of Jesus Christ in the sacrament of Holy Communion.

I know that it makes no sense developmentally for a seven-year-old child to believe in something as abstract as the presence of God in a little wafer of unleavened bread. But I did. I really believed that Jesus came to me when I received Holy Communion and I was greatly comforted by that belief. I needed something to hold on to when I was feeling powerless. My feelings of powerlessness, sadness and even fear were at their worst when my parents fought with each other and threatened to leave each other. My father even threatened to take my sister and me from my mother. I have been grateful all of my life for that priest and nun teaching me that Jesus really came to me in the sacrament of Holy Communion.

Perhaps that is why I tried to convince the adults in the United Methodist churches that I pastored years later to allow the children to come to Holy Communion. At the time, many United Methodists, and other Christians as well, believed that children were incapable of understanding what Holy Communion was all about. I tried to help the adults to understand that even a well-educated pastor doesn't understand everything about Communion. But many adults resisted letting the younger children receive this sacrament.

I did all that I could do as a pastor to teach young children

that Jesus cared about them. I encouraged the children, especially in my last full-time parish, to learn the hymn whose first verse is this: "Jesus loves me, This I know, For the Bible tells me so; Little ones to Him belong, They are weak, But He is strong." I wanted the children to know that Jesus is real and that He loves every one of them. Children, especially younger children, seem much more open to the experience of being loved by God than many of their parents are.

PUBLIC SCHOOL TEACHERS:

It's a long story about how it happened but one of the problems that I had to live with in school, as well as everywhere else, was my stuttering. Many children have a problem with stuttering for a short while when they are around three years old. For most of them it doesn't last very long. For me, it seemed to go on interminably. In fact, it lasted until I was in my twenties. Perhaps as difficult as the stuttering itself was that there was no one to help me. Most of my teachers did not even acknowledge it.

There was one exception and I met him in Lunenburg, Massachusetts. His name was Richard and he was my eighth grade history teacher. He was also the coach who gave me my first opportunity to manage a sports team.

One day when we were alone Richard spoke to me about my stuttering and he asked me to read something while he recorded my voice. He tried to figure out what letters in the alphabet that I was having difficulty pronouncing. We didn't make a lot of progress in curing my problem but at least I had someone who acknowledged my stuttering and talked about it with me. Richard helped me to feel a little less like an outsider and for that I am grateful.

Another teacher who made a real difference in my life was Robert. He was my sophomore English teacher and he did a great job introducing me to different styles of writing. He also helped me to write a speech when I was running for reelection as the class treasurer.

However, it was he did when I was a first year high school student sitting in a large study hall that I provided me with a revelatory experience. I was being not so quietly hassled by a high school junior whose name was Kenny and I didn't know how to cope. Robert walked over to our table and asked what was going on. Kenny made a comment about how socially unacceptable I was and how unlikely it was that I would have anyone as a friend. Without hesitating a moment Robert announced to Kenny and everyone else within earshot that he "would be glad to have Mr. LaPierre as a friend." That shut Kenny up. I was simply astounded that a high school teacher would say that he would be glad to have me as a friend.

That same year I learned another lesson in kindness that was not part of the curriculum. It was during a class in first year algebra that our teacher, Minerva, demonstrated that everyone deserved respect. One of the slower students got confused and tried arguing that a particular letter of the alphabet came before another. He was wrong but the teacher didn't focus on proving that he was wrong. She did assure him that he had the letters out of sequence and, when he protested, she very kindly said, "Just say your alphabet to yourself, John." Then she moved on. She modeled for me what I did not see in my father—that it was possible to correct another person's errors without humiliating them.

The next year I took a course in plane geometry. The teacher was named Jim. One day he was fingering something that was hanging on a chain around his neck. He explained to us that it was one third of a silver coin. It had been split into three pieces and each of three friends had taken a piece of the coin as a sign of their friendship. Though they had gone their own ways they were reminded of their bond through that coin. It was the first time that I had ever thought that friendship could be life long.

There was a point, however, when I had to learn a very different kind of lesson—one that had to do with limits. By then I had moved back to Leominster, Massachusetts. During my junior year I took a course in history and one in physics. Now those were perfectly normal courses to take as a junior in high school. However, I didn't behave as well as I should have in either class. I fell in with two or three other students, all of us smart, who decided to play chess during class.

The history class was taught by John. He was a very tolerant man. There was no doubt in my mind that he could hear the chess pieces rattling back and forth as we passed the portable chess set from one person to the other. However, those of us who were playing chess in his class were also earning an "A" in history. So, we were allowed to get away with our misbehavior.

Then we decided to extend our chess playing to our physics class. We played for awhile and nothing happened. So we assumed that the teacher was as tolerant as John was. We were wrong. One day, before class started, the teacher approached me and the fellow I was playing chess with and quietly said, "You gentlemen can go find another place to play chess." I was mortified. I had never been punished like this. So the other student and I headed off to the vice-principal's office. After listening to our story, he said that we could return to the physics class the next day but we had to give up playing chess in class. We did!

The other high school teacher who made a lasting impression on me was Marvin. He was our chemistry teacher and he taught us a great deal. However, one lesson stands out. Marvin taught us what is known as the "Bohr Theory of the Atom." In this theory the atom is pictured as a round ball of tiny particles known as neutrons and protons that is surrounded by a series of circles in which even smaller particles known as electrons move in orbits. After completing this explanation he then told us that when we got to college our professors would tell us that the explanation that he had just given us was all wrong. That simply astounded me. I learned from that experience that there were different levels to truth and different models or ways of explaining what we knew about reality.

COLLEGE PROFESSORS:

When I got to college there was, of course, much more to learn. During my first semester of college, when I was at St. Mary's College in Winona, Minnesota, I took a five credit course in Latin. The professor, an old Catholic monsignor, was a good teacher. Two of the phrases that he used very often stuck in my memory. The first was used at the end of class: "Exerunt omnes!" Freely translated it means "Everybody out!" The second phrase was used the day before a quiz: "Verbum sapientiae!" That one meant "A word to the wise!" and it was his only warning that there would be a quiz the next day.

Another professor who made an impression on me was our public speaking teacher. He required seven kinds of speeches including a humorous speech, a persuasive speech and a pantomime. However, it was his own example of speaking that most impressed me. I had never met a person who made such an array of uncontrollable sounds. He snorted, whistled and made other noises that I cannot describe. Then he would speak with perfect clarity in well-thought-out sentences delivered in a normal voice. I was truly amazed that he could teach public speaking given the outbursts of different sounds that he made. The rumor among the students was that he had been "shell-shocked" in the Korean Conflict. I had only the vaguest understanding of what that meant. However, I decided that, if he could teach speaking with his vocal problems, then I would not give up in my efforts to speak clearly.

After one semester I transferred to the State College in Fitchburg, Massachusetts. There I met a variety of helpful teachers. One of them, from whom I learned a great deal, was Professor Louis. I had signed up for a course entitled "American Literature II" but Professor Louis decided to make it a course on poetry. I did not like poetry in large part because I did not understand it. However, I learned to understand it enough to write several poems that were published in our college newspaper. Professor Louis opened my mind to a whole new means of expression.

The desire to learn was so strong in me that I was sure that nothing would get in the way of increasing my knowledge. However, something did get in the way—at least for a semester or two. I fell in love with the woman who is now my wife—Jane. As a result of being in love and having just learned about poetry, I sat in what is known as n-dimensional calculus writing poems to Jane. By not paying attention to that professor I got a D in the class. In fact, that semester I went from being a Dean's List student to being on academic probation. The lesson was that I had limits. I could not go to school full-time, work thirty hours a week, and write love poems in class.

After Jane and I married and I changed majors for the fourth time I finally was able to focus. The summer before I graduated I deepened my understanding of a lesson about working hard that various people, including my father, had tried to teach me for years. It was a terribly hot summer and I had signed up for eight credits of physical chemistry. The professor, whose name I have forgotten, made a point of telling us that he was Finnish and that Finns were not bothered by hot weather. In fact, he said that the hotter it got the harder he worked. I, on the other hand, hated hot weather. But I faced a choice. Either I was going to work hard in his class, despite the hot weather, or I wasn't going to get a degree in chemistry. So I worked hard.

During my final semester of college I did two terms of student teaching. I thought that I might become a public school science teacher. I had a number of interesting experiences during those two terms. The one that is burned into my memory, however, is the one where I learned how even something apparently simple doesn't always make sense to another person. It was the concept of density. The students were not the most gifted but, in this case, they were certainly my teachers.

Now, density is the mass of something divided by its volume—the amount of material that one can fit into a given space. That's all there is to it. I spent two weeks working forty minutes a day trying to teach a class of 8th graders the concept of density. I failed. Finally, I gave up and moved onto another topic. I discovered that I had a lot to learn about teaching.

A LESSON ABOUT COMMUNICATING MY IDEAS:

After I graduated from college with a degree in chemistry, I was promoted from technician to chemist at Foster Grant Co. I soon learned a new lesson about communicating.

This time the lesson involved a group of scientists. It happened when I researched an idea about monitoring a chemical process known as "polymerization" (making large molecules out of small ones). I used a laboratory instrument known as a refractometer to measure a property of the polymerizing chemical known as its "refractive index (the ratio of the speed of light going through air compared to the speed of light going through a substance)." I did the work and was convinced that the process worked. However, when I wrote the report summarizing my results I said too much about what might go wrong with the technique that I had developed and too little about what was right about it. When it didn't get implemented as part of our analytical procedures I asked the laboratory manager why. He told me that when he read my report I seemed to be saying that the technique wouldn't work. I had failed to communicate my results clearly. I worked very hard to never let that happen again.

GRADUATE SCHOOL:

While working for Foster Grant I took a graduate course with Professor Fraser. The course was directly related to what I was doing at work. It was basically a course in using microscopes to study the large molecules that are known as polymers.

It was while taking this course at the University of Massachusetts in Amherst that I learned a lesson that had nothing to do with microscopes. This one was about the competitiveness of graduate school for the professors. The professor who taught the course that I took had fifty-five papers published in journals and he was the junior person in the department in terms of publications. One professor I met in the department had published one hundred and twenty-five papers and another had two hundred and fifty! I'm certain that they each had a flock of graduate students to help in doing research and publishing papers to which the professors could attach their names. Nevertheless, these were staggering numbers.

They symbolized for me that there was an unending pecking-order not only in academia but also in industry—at least in the field of chemistry. I soon realized that I was at the bottom of the pile. It wasn't good enough to have just a bachelor's degree (which was what I had at the time) or even a master's degree in chemistry. It wasn't until one had a Ph.D. that one was ever noticed. Then there was the question of where one had studied, how many years it had taken to earn your Ph.D. and who your dissertation advisor was (i.e. how famous that person was). Then, after earning a Ph.D., there was also the question of whether one had done a post-doctoral fellowship and where. If you had done one post-doctoral fellowship had you done a second one? Of course, if you then went on to a third post-doctoral fellowship was that because you could not get a job? When a person had finally dealt with all of these questions there was still the issue, even in industry, of how many publications you had and in which journals—i.e. were they well-known journals? The lesson for me was that no one ever "arrived"—i.e. no one was ever done proving oneself. This fit with some of the lessons that my father had tried to teach me—i.e. that one has to work hard and that the "boss" (my father, the supervisor, the professor, the dissertation advisor, etc.) is never quite satisfied.

COUNSELOR EDUCATION:

Even though I achieved a moderate degree of success as a chemist I never escaped the sense that I was called to do something else with my life. While I was working at Polaroid Corporation as an analytical chemist I developed an interest in counseling. In part this was due to my experience of going through counseling for an extended period of time to learn how to cope with grief, anger and family issues. The counselor's name was Murray and he was genuinely helpful.

I decided to enroll in a counseling training program at Northeastern University. One of the people I met in my master's degree program was named Tom. He was a psychologist who taught a course on psychological testing that I took. Whatever else he taught me about testing I shall never forget a statement he made one day that summed up his approach to being a counselor. He said, "In this business (counseling) you have to be in the business of giving all of it away all of the time." I understood him to mean that a counselor must be willing to share all that she or he knew with whoever needed to know it.

There were other professors at Northeastern who made a lasting impression on me. One was Professor Irvin. Professor Irvin taught the two semester course on group counseling. I learned a great deal in that course including how anxious I was about leading a group. We all had to take turns leading a group session and I volunteered to be first. Arguably, I was the least equipped to lead a group but I wanted to get it over with. I inadvertently caused a negative reaction during the session that I led. I was the first to arrive and I greeted each person by name and welcomed them to the group. I don't recall what else I did during that session but I do recall that several people were upset that I knew their names. They expressed the feeling that they weren't sure they wanted anyone to know their names so soon. It didn't take long for me to realize that I had memorized everyone's name as a way of reducing my anxiety—i.e. I might not know anything about running a group but I could at least know the names of the people who were there.

Professor Irvin also made an impression on me by the way that he graded. Some of the students expressed the usual anxieties about grades and what it would take to earn an "A." Wanting to empower us to focus on learning and not on doing "enough" to earn a certain grade Professor Irvin offered us a deal. He offered to give us each an "A" if we would concentrate on learning the process of group counseling. We agreed. It's not clear to me whether I learned less or more than I would have learned had I been competing for a grade. But I did learn about group counseling that year and I also learned that anxiety is a problem even for counselors in training.

Another professor who made an impression on me (I've forgotten his name) was the man who led the counseling techniques courses. We learned a lot about counseling techniques including the use of what was known as Gestalt psychology. We were then asked to use our newfound knowledge in practice counseling sessions with another member of the class. I was absolutely amazed at how much anger I had in me. It poured out of me in the practice counseling sessions and the professor let it happen. He apparently recognized that it had to come out if I was going to develop as a counselor. I later went into another round of extended counseling to begin to deal with my anger and the fear that drove it.

There was at least one other person who was an important teacher before I went to seminary. He was a psychologist who taught a course at the Cambridge Center for Adult Education. By the time that I took the course it was labeled "Abnormal Psychology." However, when it was first advertised it was titled "The Psychology of Madness." That's what attracted me to it. I wanted to know what it meant to be "Mad" in the sense of being crazy.

I knew then and I know now that a lot of people don't like the term "crazy" but I also knew that a lot of people talked about others as being "crazy." When I was a child in the 1940s and 1950s I lived near what was locally known as "The Insane Asylum." The only thing I knew about being insane was that there was a dark shadow around the whole idea of being crazy. No one talked about it near me.

What the professor of the "Abnormal Psychology" course did for me was to open the door to exploring the inner world of what it was like to be "mad." He also told us very explicitly that we should use the word "crazy," at least in class, to describe people who were "crazy." He freed us to name a problem that many people would not openly name. Much later in my career as a chaplain and a therapist I learned to distinguish many kinds of mental illness based upon their symptoms. I also learned that calling someone "crazy" is not helpful. It is generally demeaning. But, for its time, the course was a liberating experience.

SEMINARY PROFESSORS:

Five years after I completed the M.Ed. in counseling I entered seminary for the third time. This time I would complete the program and earn a Master of Divinity degree. The professors all had a lot to offer but several stand out.

One was Professor Stephen. He was my Old Testament professor. Besides what I learned from him about the Old Testament I also learned a great deal about prayer. He was the only professor who prayed before each class. I have listened to a number of people pray, including many clergy, but I have never heard anyone pray like Stephen. When he prayed I had the sense that I was listening to a person pour out his heart to the Almighty. It is hard to express the degree of intimacy and openness that I experienced in his prayers. Suffice it to say that I treasured every experience of overhearing Stephen pray.

Another professor who made a lasting impression on me was Professor Walter. He taught courses on preaching and on prayer and he supervised students who were placed in churches for internships or for preaching assignments on a week-by-week basis. I took his courses on preaching and prayer and benefited from them. The course on prayer may have offered me the most insight into the soul of this professor. During that course he read a poem by Francis Thompson entitled "The Hound of Heaven." The "Hound of Heaven" was a metaphor for God and it portrayed God as One who pursues us down the corridors of time and space because of God's great love for each of us. While reciting that poem to us Professor Walter literally wept as he recited the parts of the poem that had to do with God pursuing each of us out of love. I don't remember anyone being so moved by the experience of God's nearness that she or he wept. His faith was obviously integrated to the depths of his soul.

The other way that Professor Walter affected my life was by what he said to me one night in the seminary library. I don't know what others might have said to him about my growing frustration with the seminary's lack of emphasis on the spiritual development of its students. Whatever he had heard, Professor Walter walked over to me one night and simply said, "Don't let them get to you." My belief was that God spoke to me through that professor to keep me from leaving the seminary. I heeded his advice.

Another professor who made a significant impact on my learning was Professor Marvin. I took four courses in ethics from him and I learned a lot about ethics. But he gave us something much more important than information. He encouraged us to learn how to ask the right questions. I intuitively realized, as a scientist, that it is not possible to find the answers to a problem until one learns to ask the right questions. Professor Marvin helped us to learn to ask the right questions as we explored ethical dilemmas.

He also taught me something that continues to help me on an emotional level as well as other ways. One day we were discussing anger in one of his classes. He said to us, "Anger is the normal reaction to injustice." Of course, it is but I didn't know that! I had never been given permission to recognize anger as a normal reaction. It was always either a sin or dangerous to my well-being (at home as a child). Professor Marvin's comment freed me to admit that I was angry when there was an injustice being committed. Only after I recognized what I was feeling could I choose the best way to react.

The professor who taught "Systematic Theology" taught many of us an entirely different kind of lesson. She was demanding and rigorous in her thinking and that was good. However, she was amazingly critical—especially of our papers. I have written many papers, at all levels of education and many for publication in journals and magazines, but I have never found anyone to be as critical as her. Professor Leslie seemed to write as much in red ink on the back of each page of my papers as I had typed in black ink on the front. It was hard to make sense of getting a "B" on a ten page paper with ten pages of critical comments and questions in red ink. At the very least I learned that in the seminary one has to be able to support any statement that one makes that has theological content.

One final comment is about my professor of New Testament. Professor Burton was an acknowledged expert in his field and I took five courses that he taught. I learned several lessons from him. One of the most important arose when we were talking about the end of the Gospel according to John. There is debate among scholars about whether the author of the first twenty chapters of this Gospel is the same person who wrote chapter 21. Professor Burton, after exploring the issue thoroughly, said "If it has functioned as Scripture for most of the last twenty centuries then why not treat it as Scripture?" That seemed to be a liberating and tolerant way to deal with Scripture.

OTHER TEACHERS:

Along with the teachers in the various educational institutions I attended there have been people who became my teachers in non-classroom settings. One of them was a man whose name I have forgotten. I went to high school with him for a year. This man served a tour of combat in Vietnam. I met him after he returned from combat. He told me the story of his first full day home from Vietnam. He came downstairs on a Saturday morning and heard the sound of gunfire. He rolled down the rest of the stairs looking for cover and reaching for a weapon to return fire. There was no actual threat. His younger brother had been watching the Saturday morning cartoons and there had apparently been some shooting in the cartoon. It was a lesson both in what we are teaching children through some of the cartoons as well as a lesson in at least one of the adjustments that combat veterans have to make when they return to civilian life.

Another lesson was taught to me by a man who was a neighbor during my first year at Bangor Theological Seminary in Bangor, Maine. Royce and I got to know each other because his car battery lost its charge on cold winter nights in Maine and I had a battery charger which would restore life to his battery for a few days.

During our visits Royce shared with me how his life had fallen apart after he had completed his tour of duty in the Air Force. He had been divorced three times and was an alcoholic. He could not hold a job. He attributed the chaos in his life to the time in 1971 that he spent as part of the crew in a B-52 bomber. Although the plane flew at fifty thousand feet and Royce could not see the devastation caused by the plane's bombs, he "knew" the havoc that they were causing to the people of North Vietnam. It troubled him deeply and he could never escape the thoughts of the harm that those bombs caused. It was another reminder of what war does to the veterans as well as to the victims.

Another teacher was a man I met during my first year in seminary. He was a chaplain at a mental health treatment facility near the seminary. I met Rev. Scott because I wanted to do a supervised internship with mentally ill people. To put it bluntly, I wanted to learn more about what mentally ill people are like.

One of the first lessons I needed to learn occurred shortly after I arrived for my Friday afternoon training sessions. He had assigned me to the Forensics Unit—a ward for people judged to be "criminally insane." I was quite anxious about how to cope with this population. None of my training in counseling had prepared me for dealing with people with this combination of problems. After reporting on my initial difficulties in knowing how to approach or talk to people on this ward, Rev. Scott told me to buy and wear a cross (i.e. I am a Christian and it would be appropriate to wear one.) when I was on duty as a student chaplain.

For reasons that were not apparent to me at the time I resisted the idea (I rather suspect that I reacted to Rev. Scott as if he were my father.). In fact, Rev. Scott and I ended up in a near-shouting match over his suggestion. Finally, I gave in and purchased a cross. Rev. Scott had been right. It made all the difference in how the patients related to me. They instantly accorded me the title of "Chaplain." I was amazed at how it opened doors for people to acknowledge why I was there and sometimes even to share some of their story with me. I have worn a cross ever since.

One other teacher of note was a man named Michael. I met him during one of my assignments as a church pastor. He was an alcohol counselor at a nearby hospital. I brought one of our children to him because I thought that this teenager had a problem with alcohol. Michael interviewed me. Then he interviewed our child. Then he spoke to me again. Michael said to me, "Your child does not have a drinking problem but you need a group!"

I was stunned. I had brought our child in thinking that I was doing the right thing to help this child to cope with a drinking problem and I needed a group? Well, Michael was right. I had grown up in an alcoholic home and it had left me with a number of emotional problems. I joined a group known as "Adult Children of Alcoholics" and attended faithfully every week for four years. It proved to be a healing experience. Michael had taught me a valuable lesson. The people in the "Adult Children of Alcoholics" (ACOA) groups helped me to learn many more.

One of the lessons that the ACOA groups helped me to learn is that those of us who grow up in alcoholic families have a tremendous fear of abandonment. I recognized that was true for me. What I also had to learn was that those of us who grow up in alcoholic families will do anything to avoid the pain of abandonment.

Another teacher whom I met in that same parish assignment was Rev. George. George was the pastor of a neighboring parish in town and had far greater experience in pastoral ministry than I had. One day I went to him for advice. I shared with him how a small but vocal minority of parishioners in one of the two churches that I served was complaining about the comments that I made about politics during my sermons. I didn't know what to say to them. George smiled and picked up a Bible and simply said, "Larry, if they took all of the politics out of this book it would be a very slim volume indeed." That helped me to regain the confidence that I needed to continue to address some of the political issues of the day in my sermons.

Perhaps one of my greatest teachers was a woman named Barbara. She was the organist of one of the churches I served in Vermont. She was a gentle soul and seemed to always be pleasant. One day she told me the story of how she had been forced out of her position as choir director by another member of the congregation. She spoke of this experience with some sadness but no bitterness. She refused to allow someone else's actions to change her from the pleasant person that she was. I still have a long ways to go in being as gentle and forgiving as she was.

The greatest teacher I have ever encountered was and is my wife Jane. She has taught me countless lessons but I will cite one that is obviously relevant to parish ministry. I had gone to visit a dying parishioner in her home on the Down East coast of Maine. We had a productive visit and, at the end of the visit, she asked me if I would bring her purse to her. She could not move very easily. I agreed to do so with a sinking feeling in my stomach. She reached into her purse and gave me a five-dollar bill. I didn't know what to do. To refuse would have been unkind. To accept it would leave me in the position of accepting money for what I was already being paid to do.

I accepted the money with a great deal of anxiety and I immediately went home and discussed the situation with Jane. She asked me if I would have accepted cookies from the woman if she had offered them to me and I said, "Of course." Then Jane pointed out that the woman could not walk very easily and thus could not bake any cookies for me. She gave me what she had—some money. I needed to learn to accept small gifts and be gracious about doing so.

Another teacher was a funeral director named Virgil. When I met him in 1980 he had been the local funeral director for several decades. One day he told me a story. Actually, he told me several stories but this one was about a meeting that occurred in a particular town along the coast of Maine. It happened in 1976. A fleet of black Cadillacs and Lincolns arrived in town and went to a local restaurant. According to Virgil the Mafia had held a meeting at the restaurant to divide up the coast of Maine into territories for various Mafia families to control the transporting of illegal drugs. It made me wonder which, if any, of the people I knew were involved in the local drug trade. It also made me realize that there was nowhere to escape from the presence of organized crime.

I also learned a great deal from my experience of being a student pastor in that Down East parish in Maine. One of the lessons was that there were kind people in that parish despite the fact that the leadership of that parish was glad to see me leave at the end of my two years. I had frustrated them dozens of times with my attempts to work with them according to the rules laid out in what is known as <u>The Book of Discipline of The United Methodist Church</u>. All three churches were United Methodist churches but they chafed at the rules imposed by the denomination as well as at my way of leading them.

During the last week of my tenure there I experienced some remarkable acts of generosity. One family gave me twenty dollars. That was 1982 and it would be equivalent to nearly fifty dollars today. More importantly, this family had no income because the husband had lost his job due to state budget cutbacks and his spouse stayed at home with their young children. There literally were no jobs for a radius of at least eighteen miles unless one already had the money to operate a lobster boat or a shrimp dragger and they didn't. They were living off of the money that he had withdrawn from his state pension fund. I still struggle to be as generous as that family was to me.

During that same week, on the very day we moved, another family also gave me twenty dollars. These folks were quite poor as well. I had also had a major theological disagreement with the matriarch of their family. But that dispute healed and they were the only family to help us to load the truck as we prepared to move to my new parish assignment. They embodied the reality of forgiveness and generosity.

I have not always been ready to learn but when I have been ready to learn there have always been teachers close by.

CHAPTER 5
—COLLEAGUES IN MINISTRY

During my years in pastoral ministry I was guided by many professional colleagues. They included clergy, funeral directors, nurses, physicians and others, some of whom I have already alluded to, who helped me to discover what it meant to be first a pastor and later a hospital chaplain.

Even before I was assigned to a student parish I was challenged to express my sense of identity by a minister named Lynne. She had special training in hospital ministry (i.e. she was a Clinical Pastoral Education supervisor) and thus was a good observer of human behavior. She was charged with guiding the United Methodist seminarians at Bangor Theological Seminary. When she interviewed me she asked me a deceptively simple question: "Who are you?" I was stunned at the implications of that question. It caused me a moment of panic as I wondered "Who am I?" Finally, I answered with the simplest truth that I could find: "I'm a man in transition."

And so I was. A few weeks earlier (in 1979) I had been a senior engineer with a staff of five people charged with the responsibility of supporting a manufacturing line producing integrated circuits on silicon wafers ("chips"). I was well paid and I had a demonstrated record of competence as a scientist. At the seminary I was a graduate student with no income and I was treated by several of the faculty as if I knew nothing of consequence about ministry. They might even have been right but it was difficult to accept. Rev. Lynne's question once again reminded me that I probably needed to make more changes in my ways of dealing with people especially as I prepared for pastoral ministry.

STUDENT PASTOR:

After the first year in seminary I was appointed to a student pastorate consisting of three small United Methodist churches along the Down East coast of Maine. There I met a number of colleagues who were helpful to me.

One of the kindest was a Disciples of Christ minister whose last name I can't remember. Don, as most of us knew him, pastored the only Disciples of Christ parish in Maine at that time. It happened to be in Lubec, Maine six miles from where I pastored a church in West Lubec. Don worked hard at sustaining an ecumenical openness amongst the churches of Lubec. He organized ecumenical worship services in Lubec and was the driving force behind a volunteer chaplaincy program at the hospital thirty miles away in Machias.

Perhaps what I will remember him the most for was the fact that he died doing a wedding. Some of you who are reading this book may think, "Oh, how awful, especially during a wedding!" From one point of view it wasn't all that awful. He simply had a heart attack while doing what he loved the most—being a pastor. Don was over eighty years old and had been in ministry over forty years in the same town. The bride was not from Don's parish and, as it happened, her pastor was present for the ceremony. Don had already signed the certificate. So the bride's pastor finished the ceremony after Don was taken to the hospital. I greatly admire him for staying in ministry in Lubec for so many years. I suspect that his perseverance may have been motivated, in part, by the difficulty of convincing another Disciples of Christ minister to come to Maine to replace him. Nevertheless, Don was dedicated and set a wonderful example for those of us who were younger pastors.

While pastoring the three churches east of Machias I had an experience in ecumenicity that I never expected. We had two or three ecumenical services a year that rotated amongst the churches. One year I was invited to preach at a Good Friday service. There was nothing unusual about that except that the service that year (1981) was in the Catholic church in Machias. I preached on the Suffering Servant Song in Isaiah 52:12-53:13. It was a text that resonated within that Catholic community and the message was well-received. As a former Catholic I really appreciated the opportunity to preach in a Catholic church.

Another pastor in that area reminded me, however, of the constant presence of intolerance amongst some clergy. I called this man to invite him to join the clergy group that met for breakfast once a month at the well-known Helen's Restaurant. His response was negative. When I encouraged him to come at least once and meet us he wanted to know whether I was "saved." This is code language in many conservative Christian churches for "Have you accepted Jesus Christ as your personal Savior?" Typically, one's answer is not only supposed to be "Yes" but also to name the exact date and preferably the location where it happened. I told him that, if he would allow me to explain what I meant, that my answer was, "Yes, I have been saved." But he wasn't interested in hearing my story. He treated me like I was an outcast. It was a lesson in how far we as Christians have to go to become "one in Christ."

My (United Methodist) pastoral colleague, Bob, was stationed eighteen miles west and south of me in the town of Columbia Falls. He helped me with his humorous stories about ministry. He also told me a story that involved some perseverance. One Christmas Eve he arrived in one of the churches he was pastoring to discover that there was no heat in the church. The oil tank had literally run dry and the temperature both inside and outside the church was zero degrees.

They don't teach us how to deal with these situations in our seminary classes—probably because there are too many of these unpredictable occurrences. The bottom line is that Bob led a Christmas Eve service—a very cold and a very short Christmas Eve service. It was twenty minutes long to be exact but at least the people had a service.

FULL-TIME PASTORATES:

In my first full-time parish, in Lincoln and Mattawamkeag, Maine, I met a very welcoming ecumenical clergy group. We met monthly for breakfast and we organized five ecumenical services a year that rotated from Lincoln to Lee to Mattawamkeag, Maine. I was the preacher at these services more than half of the time because I like to preach.

One All Saints Day (November 1), however, I needed help from my colleagues. I was hospitalized in Intensive Care with an irregular heart rhythm. I was scheduled to preach that evening at an ecumenical service. The sermon was written but I couldn't be there to preach it. A Roman Catholic nun, whose name I can't recall, volunteered to preach my sermon for me. I truly appreciated her willingness to help.

One of the lessons that I slowly assimilated from my time in Lincoln and Mattawamkeag was how divided the Christian Church really is. I knew that, of course, from my experience with ecumenical discussion groups, from comments that my mother made about the Protestant churches she knew in her youth and from the diversity of the churches that I had encountered in the many places we had lived.

However, it slowly dawned on me that the little town of Lincoln, a town of about five thousand people, had a disproportionate number of churches even given the diversity in Christian denominations. There were twelve churches when I arrived and thirteen when I left. There were four mainline churches (Roman Catholic, Episcopal, Congregational and United Methodist) and nine other churches divided between Baptists and Pentecostals. I was amazed that the town needed so many small Baptist and Pentecostal churches but apparently the congregations kept dividing over points of doctrine.

Over the years I have come to believe that a lot of this divisiveness happens because people are afraid to be wrong about doctrine. It's as if we believe that if we don't get all of the teachings exactly right that we will be condemned to an eternity of misery when we die. So, we create new congregations in an attempt to preserve the truth as we know it.

This expectation that the essential core of the truth about God could be found was reinforced by a physician one night in the hospital in Lincoln. His name was Scott and he and I were there to see the same very ill patient. While we were waiting for something to change the physician saw my Bible. He asked to look at it and, of course, I gave it to him. He proceeded to open the Bible to specific passages, read them and then ask me whether I believed these passages. I finally realized that I was being evaluated on my faith stance to see if I was one of those who would be accepted as one of "us" or whether I would be rejected as one of "them"—"them" being the outsiders, the unbelievers, the ones who would almost surely go to Hell.

To be fair to this physician, he took excellent care of me as my personal physician. It is a long story but the bottom line was that he diagnosed me with a heart problem in 1983. Finally, in 1984, when I was admitted to the Intensive Care Unit with an irregular heartbeat, Dr. Scott and another physician decided that I needed a heart catheterization (a procedure to examine the inside of the arteries in the heart). After it was all over and I was given a clean bill of health I told Dr. Scott that I had been praying for him while he was caring for me. He shocked me by responding that he had been praying for me. Never before or since has a physician told me that. It was wonderful to know that he prayed for his patients.

Another lesson from a colleague came by way of my District Superintendent. In The United Methodist Church (UMC) this is a person who supervises upwards of seventy pastors and the churches to which they are assigned. S/He is the bishop's representative in a geographical district. His name was Richard and he was helpful to me in understanding the financial issues that the Lincoln UMC, where I was the pastor, was undergoing. As was true in many small churches we were having difficulty raising enough money to cover budgeted expenses. Yet, when it came time to do some work on the parsonage, the money flowed in. Richard simply said, "You can always raise money for buildings." It seems as if people feel better about investing in something that is tangible than in something less visible like the oil bill.

When I got to Vermont I, once again, found a friendly, supportive ecumenical clergy group in Swanton. We, too, sponsored several services a year. The most moving for me was the Good Friday service. During that service the four congregations in town and their pastors took part in brief services that were held in each of the four parishes. As we walked from church to church, each pastor took a turn carrying a large wooden cross made of 2" x 8" pine lumber that was big enough to put a medium-size man or woman on. It was also big enough to give us a limited sense of how difficult it must have been for Jesus to carry his cross. I found it to be a tiring and yet spiritually uplifting experience to carry that cross to the church I pastored. It was the only one of the five parishes I served where that kind of procession occurred.

Another experience with the openness of the local clergy happened when I was approached by a member of Memorial United Methodist Church in Swanton. Debbie wanted to marry her long-time fiancé John. John was a Roman Catholic and wanted to be married by a priest. Debbie wanted to be married in her church. The solution to the problem was found when the local Catholic pastor agreed to perform the marriage with me in the church that I pastored. We each did half of the service and everyone seemed pleased. It was the second time that I had co-officiated at an ecumenical wedding with a Catholic priest. The first was a year earlier in Maine when the local Catholic pastor (in Howland) and I co-officiated at the wedding of our son Jim and his then fiancée Brigitte.

Another experience of supportiveness and ecumenical openness occurred one day when I attended the funeral for one of our neighbors. I was there simply to pay my respects to my neighbor. The Catholic priest who was officiating that day was from St. Anne's Shrine in Isle LaMotte, Vermont. He learned that I was in the congregation and immediately asked me to join him in a room set aside for clergy. He greeted me warmly and immediately insisted that I co-officiate with him at the funeral. I appreciated his warmth and genuine desire to have me assist in the service.

It reminded me again that God is at work in all of the churches trying to bring us together.

I would not have been able to cope with the challenges of pastoral ministry if my colleagues, family and friends had not been supporting me as I gradually responded to the call into ordained ministry.

CHAPLAINCY:

I have already mentioned the role that the Rev. Dr. Stan played in telling me about the part-time opening for a Protestant Chaplain at the VA hospital in Vermont. Because of the direct encouragement of my supervisor, Rev. Dr. Bill, I was later able to later apply for and be named as the Chief Chaplain at this hospital. Without Bill's support this would surely not have happened.

However, there were several other people who made my growth in chaplaincy possible. One of them was a Clinical Pastoral Education (CPE) supervisor—Rev. Scott. I enrolled in my first unit of CPE in the Fall of 1989. (My third unit of CPE, which I also did under his leadership, was about a year later.) My principal goal in that first unit was to learn how to listen more effectively to people. I thought that I had already had a significant amount of training in listening. However, my problem was that I didn't often get around to using my skill in listening because I was so busy talking. It was partly because I was so opinionated (on a good day one might say informed) and partly because I was so defensive. If I kept talking then I didn't have to hear the negative feedback that I apparently was afraid was just waiting to be delivered.

Rev. Scott helped me to realize that I talked too much to really listen effectively. However, it was difficult to come to this realization. In part, this was because I had a transferential reaction (an unconscious experience) to Scott. I reacted to him as if he was my father. I doubt that I have resolved all of that transference and I doubt that I listen enough. However, I am conscious of the need to talk less so that others can talk more and be heard.

A second CPE supervisor, Rev. Carol, was very helpful to me in working on my continued growth in ministry as a chaplain. She asked me to read a book on dealing with anger. I think that she asked at least some of the other people in the program that summer to read the same book. However, I knew that I needed to read the book because I had had a problem with being angry for a very long time. One of the other gifts that Rev. Carol gave to me was the sense that when she asked me how I was doing she really wanted to know. With her help during the unit of CPE that she led I was able to accept a significant amount of critical feedback about my practice of ministry without being overwhelmed.

Of course, both Rev. Scott and Rev. Carol could have been included in the chapter on teachers. However, I chose to include them in this chapter because, in fact, we became colleagues when my training was completed. Even during the time when I was enrolled in the three units of CPE they were colleagues because we were working in hospitals that were affiliated with the Dartmouth Medical School system.

There were many other colleagues at the VA hospital in Vermont who helped me to develop as a chaplain. A psychologist, Dr. John, was one of them. John accepted me as a colleague in treating the psycho-social-spiritual needs of the veterans. He referred patients to me and we often collaborated on how to best help particular patients.

Another psychologist, a man whose name I have forgotten, invited me at the recommendation of the patients in his group to join the group as a co-leader once a month. My presence there was to facilitate dealing with the connections between psychological and spiritual dimensions of the veterans' experiences. After I had met with the group for some time, this psychologist encouraged me to write a paper about my experiences dealing with spirituality of these veterans. That paper was eventually published in *The Journal of Religion and Health*.

One other psychologist, Dr. Alan, did more than collaborate with me in the treatment of patients. He also did the computerized statistical analysis of over six thousand pieces of data that I had accumulated for my doctoral thesis at Boston University. Without Alan's help I don't know how I would have gotten all of that data analyzed.

Nurses were also very instrumental in my training. Elaine, Lorraine, Janet, Julia and Jennifer, to name but a few, invited me to intervene in times of crisis in their patients' lives. Of course, they always asked the patient or the family first, but they very intentionally asked me to deal with the spiritual needs of patients and families especially when a patient was dying.

I have many examples of times when they called me to come into their units. One that stands out was in the medical intensive care unit. A young man was dying of an infection that could not be stopped and his partner was with him. The dying man was so sick that he could not talk. However, the nurses later told me that when I walked in the room and identified myself as a chaplain that the monitors indicated that the patient immediately relaxed. Although he died later that evening credit should go to Janet, who like many other nurses, trusted me with the spiritual care of their patients.

One final acknowledgment of the contribution of a colleague involves a prison chaplain. Rev. Dan was a chaplain in a prison in the northeast part of the country where men served long prison sentences. I asked him to find volunteers amongst the prison population who would take the several tests that I used in my doctoral research. My goal was to determine whether any of these tests, including the one based on my theory of spirituality, could distinguish between samples of various populations such as prisoners, veterans and other groups. With Chaplain Dan's help I was able to get the sample of prisoners that I needed.

Truly, these colleagues, among many others have helped me to do the work of ministry in a variety of settings.

CHAPTER 6
—PARISHIONERS

As noted earlier, some lessons cannot be learned at the seminary. They are best learned from people who attend the worship services and other activities of the local churches. I am grateful for each of the people in the churches where I preached who taught me lessons about how to be a pastor.

SUPPLY PREACHING ASSIGNMENTS:

When a church pastor is not available in Maine, and there is no church deacon, retired pastor or other person available to lead worship, the church will often turn to the seminary for a person to lead their Sunday service. This is known as "supply preaching" because the seminary is supplying the church with a preacher. Both students and professors are willing to take on this task. I supplied at several churches before I was appointed to my student parish.

Even one-time assignments offer the opportunity to learn from a congregation. Perhaps the first lesson that I learned about pastoral ministry happened in the Spring of 1980. It was in the town of Millbridge—one of many small towns along the Down East coast of Maine. After completing the worship service I was greeting parishioners at the door when an older woman said to me, "You have your deacon's voice." I assumed that she meant that I had a good voice for preaching. Then she went on to say, "That one they (the seminary) sent last week isn't going to make it." She didn't elaborate about her judgment but she didn't back down from it either. As it turned out the student who had preached the previous Sunday did leave the seminary not very long after her remarks. I realized then that some churchgoers have real insight into the capabilities of their preachers and that I could and should learn from them.

One of the most important lessons that I learned in this same period occurred in the town of Robbinston, Maine. This church was a long way from seminary. In fact, it was one hundred and twenty-five miles from the seminary along secondary and back roads. I thought that I had planned the trip very carefully in terms of timing but I took a wrong turn just before the church. By the time I corrected my error and arrived at the church I was two minutes late. As I walked into the church the lay leader of the church was walking down the aisle to start the service. The lesson? Be on time!

A third lesson was summed up years later by a man I was talking with after worship. He said, "I always start my trips the same way—with a full tank of gas and an empty bladder!" As I learned the hard way, a lot of country churches do not have bathrooms.

Another lesson that is applicable to supply preaching was taught to me by my older son. He is not gifted with a sense of direction. So he often has to stop to ask directions at a country store. He learned to buy a package of hard candy whenever he went into a store to ask for directions. He got more information that way! I adopted that practice years later when I was supply preaching in small churches in remote parts of Maine and Vermont.

STUDENT PARISH—MACHIAS, ME:

The outgoing pastor of what was to become my student pastorate taught me a lesson that every United Methodist pastor who serves a small church should learn. He simply said, "Don't upset the United Methodist Women (UMW). They pay your salary!" I soon realized how right Steve was as I looked over the sources of income for each of the three churches that I was appointed to serve. The UMW supplied about half of the cash flow of each of the three churches.

Another lesson about parish life has to do with family connections. I had come to be interviewed by the pastoral relations committee of what would become my student parish but the process wasn't moving along very well. At some point my wife Jane mentioned that her grandfather (Fred Gooch) had been born in East Machias near one of the churches in this student parish. The meeting came to an immediate halt while everyone began asking whether anyone remembered Fred Gooch. After awhile someone remembered his family and someone else remembered which road he had grown up on. From that point on the interview was a formality. I am convinced that I was hired because of my wife's grandfather.

A very important lesson about the sociology of rural Maine was taught to me by an older couple named Katherine and Ken. They had lived in their home for fifty years. However, Katherine had not been born in that town. Instead, she was born in a village just six miles from where they lived. But she had never felt accepted by the people who were native to the town where they spent their married lives. From her experience

I learned that there are two kinds of people in Maine, especially eastern Maine. There are those who were born "here," wherever "here" is, and there are those from "away." "Away" is whatever distance the local residents choose to define it as. In Katherine's experience "away" was six miles. She never overcame that barrier even after fifty years.

Another woman helped me by calling me the night before my first funeral. Annie lived in Lubec and played the organ at the church I served in West Lubec. I had not been called by the funeral director but he had put my name in the local paper as officiating at the funeral. Suspecting that I had not been told Annie called to make sure that I would be there. It was one of many reminders that parishioners can help a new pastor if s/he will just listen to them.

There was another woman in West Lubec who helped me without realizing it. Shirley was always present at the Sunday night service. She taught me two lessons. One was that it is possible to be cheerful even in the midst of difficult circumstances. I not only saw that she was cheerful at church. I visited her and saw a home that by any standards would have been described as bare and impoverished. When I stepped into her home the walls had only the outer layer of boards with the studs exposed and no insulation in the walls. Downstairs, at least, the only sheetrock I saw was in the kitchen. Shirley and her husband had what was the known as an "end heater"—a wood-fired stove box that was attached to the kitchen stove. It was the only source of heat in their home. There was much more that was lacking but Shirley did not let her poverty drag her spirits down.

Shirley also said something one night after worship that helped me to feel more appreciated. She said to my wife, "He always leaves us (the parishioners) with something to think about." I knew intuitively that I wasn't giving my parishioners all that they needed. I was too exhausted from being a full-time student and a part-time pastor to be creative in finding ways to apply the Biblical lessons to their lives. I built most of my sermons around what is known as "exegesis" which is the meaning of the text when it was written. Yet Shirley was able to hear and appreciate something in my sermons that I couldn't hear.

There was a third woman in that same parish who taught me another lesson. This one was painful. It started with a teaching moment, a brief explanation that is not as long as a sermon, of The United Methodist Church's stance on the homosexual lifestyle. I quoted from "The United Methodist Reporter," a newspaper that reported the news of The United Methodist Church. The story concerned a gay United Methodist minister in the early 1980s who either admitted to or was accused of living in a homosexual relationship. I quoted from a text in St. Paul's Letter to the Romans (1:18-32) that listed homosexuality, along with a number of other disapproved behaviors. I appealed for compassion and, to make my point that we are all sinners and have no right to judge each other harshly, I simply said, "If my sin isn't homosexuality it's in that list somewhere." By today's standards it was an insensitive remark because I left room for the practice of homosexuality to be classified as sin. I now don't believe it is.

But that wasn't the problem at the time. The problem began the following Sunday when half of the congregation of the West Lubec United Methodist Church wasn't in church. I didn't get the point at first. Then it began to dawn on me that it was the members of one extended family who were not present. Finally, it was confirmed when a daughter-in-law of the matriarch of the clan spoke to my wife in the laundromat and told her that "Granny is mad at Larry, and he needs to go talk with her."

I dutifully made an appointment to visit "Granny" and went to her home to find out what was wrong. I discovered that my "teaching moment" had upset her. She admonished me by saying, "My Bible says that homosexuality is wrong." The truth was that I had no counter argument. I didn't know enough to offer alternative explanations to help reinterpret the texts that speak about homosexuality. I forget exactly what I said but I basically repented of what I had said in church. I knew that she would keep her extended family out of church until I at least agreed not to make an issue of accepting homosexuals. I didn't go to the other extreme of declaring their lifestyle sinful. I just basically stopped talking about it in worship. The matriarch decided to allow her family to return to church. It wasn't a good solution but it was the best that I could do at the time.

Yet another lesson that I apparently needed to learn came one Sunday morning in the coastal town of Cutler. I forget what I preached on that morning but it had something to do with Jeremiah. On the way out someone noted that I had preached a prophetic sermon. I thanked the person for their remark but they weren't done. The person responded to me, "Don't forget what they did to the prophets." I was properly chastened. Indeed, I realized that if I wanted to preach prophetic sermons that I should expect a prophet's reception.

There is one final story from this period in my ministry and it was told to me by a professor of English at the local branch of the University of Maine. I didn't know this man. We met each other for the first time as we were both out for a walk. He asked me if he could tell me a story. I said, "Sure."

He then told me about a town somewhere that had been holding its town meeting in the same manner every year for as long as anyone could remember. At these meetings the moderator would read an article (a proposal) from the list of topics to be discussed that night. Then someone would make a motion and another person would second the motion.

There would be some discussion and finally a vote. Thus it had been for a long time.

One night at the town meeting business was going along as usual until a particular article was read. The moderator waited for a motion but there was no motion. The moderator read the article again and waited for a motion. There was no motion. Finally, someone in the audience stood up and asked, "Will someone please tell me why this article is so controversial?"

All of a sudden two years of unending struggle with the three churches in my student pastorate fell into place. I was from the cities of Massachusetts where some cultural groups were incredibly outspoken in voicing their feelings and expectations. I was also fresh from eighteen years in industry where, if one did not speak up, one's ideas did not get adopted.

The people whom I had been sent to pastor were from an entirely different cultural background. In their world people did not voice their demands or expectations because someone might get upset. After they got upset they would probably tell their family and then the whole family would be upset with the person who voiced their expectations too plainly. As more than one of my parishioners over the years has reminded me, "You (pastors) come and go. We have to live here."

I had come full of ideas and I was all-too-willing to verbalize my desires and expectations. I even quoted from The Book of Discipline of The United Methodist Church to support my views. I did just about everything wrong because I did not realize what my parishioners' cultural values were. Specifically, I did not listen to the "sound of silence." I assumed that my parishioners' lack of response to my ideas was either indifference or acceptance. It never occurred to me that they were just seething with resentment at my way of doing things.

I appreciate that professor's story. It helped me in five subsequent parishes in New England. It's unlikely that I will ever know whether that man set out to find me or whether our meeting, at least on a conscious level, was accidental. I do believe that God was at work in bringing us together that afternoon just a few days before I left for my new parish assignment.

LINCOLN AND MATTAWAMKEAG, MAINE:

When I got to my next parish in Lincoln and Mattawamkeag, Maine I quickly realized that I had even more lessons to learn from my parishioners. One of those parishioners was named Margaret. Being the lay leader of the church she was a member of almost all of the committees of the church in Lincoln. From time to time she missed a meeting. Then her absence became more frequent and I asked, I thought in a solicitous, compassionate manner, if anything was wrong.

She then told me what was wrong and I realized that I had been too intrusive. The lesson did not stop there. She went on to tell me that her family doctor had said to her, "Margaret, there is something wrong with every person." I have thought about that physician's comment and I have certainly found it to be true. I learned that I need to be sensitive to the possibilities of causing pain by intruding into a person's life when they are not ready to talk about their problems.

Sometime early in my pastorate of the Lincoln and Mattawamkeag United Methodist Churches I was presented with another learning opportunity. I had just finished worship and was at the back of the church greeting people. An older lady walked up to me and, as I greeted her, she said, "What do you think of alcoholics?"

Well, there were a lot of people in line that morning and I'm sure that some of them heard her question. I didn't know what they thought about the question. I only knew that I had to give this woman an honest answer without launching into a lecture. She didn't want that. She wanted to know what I thought about alcoholics.

I gave her the only answer I had then. It turns out that it is the only answer that I have now. I said, "God loves alcoholics as much as anyone else and alcoholics are as welcome in this church as anyone else." She later told me that she appreciated my answer. She also told me some of the stories of what sounded like a life filled with suffering. As a result of our conversation that day, Georgianna began to attend church regularly. She even joined the United Methodist Women's group (UMW).

In the other church in this parish, a lady named Lois taught me a small but very important lesson. I had developed the habit of prefacing my comments on a subject by saying, "In my opinion . . . ." One day Lois took me aside and said, "Larry, you don't need to say 'In my opinion.' We all know it's your opinion." That was another lesson that I didn't learn in seminary.

In this same small church a woman named Mary helped me through a crisis that developed during worship. As I was leading worship a man appeared at the back of the door uncertain about whether to interrupt or not. Sensing a problem I invited the man to come in and deliver his message. He announced that Opal's house was on fire. She was momentarily stunned and then left the worship service. I had been in the middle of the sermon and, after offering a prayer for Opal, was unclear about what I should do next. That's when Mary spoke up and gently said to me, "Larry, it's a good sermon but maybe we could have it another time. We should move on." I appreciated her suggestion and finished the service. Mary helped me to realize that there were times when I had to let go, in this case of the sermon, and deal with the crisis at hand.

Mary also shared a story that strengthened my belief that there is a reality to the spiritual world. We had gathered for Bible study when she told the story of seeing her grandmother. This would not have been unusual except that her grandmother had been dead for some time. Mary was sleeping and she awoke to see her grandmother standing at the foot of her bed. Her grandmother said nothing. She just smiled. The visit was brief. No one in the group seemed surprised that this happened. I wasn't so much surprised as I was edified. I was pleased to hear a story about the existence of a spiritual world from a person as credible as Mary. I added it to my store of lessons that I continued to learn from my parishioners.

A young optometrist in the area offered me another opportunity to learn how to be a pastor. I was in his office for an eye exam one day when he shared with me how frustrated he was with not being able to do more for his patients. He appeared to be a competent, caring professional and I wondered what I could say to help him. Then I remembered a seminar on healing that Jane and I had attended about five years earlier. There is much more to the story but the bottom line was that I remembered the seminar leader, Barbara Schlemon, R.N., telling us that, if we didn't know how else to pray for a sick person we could always pray for healing in body, in mind, in spirit and in relationships. So I suggested to the optometrist that he pray for his patients. The optometrist was open to my suggestion and I learned that I could make a difference by suggesting that a healthcare provider pray for her/his patients.

SWANTON & WEST SWANTON, VT.:

When I moved to Vermont to be a pastor I had a much different kind of learning experience. Within a few days of arriving at the church in Swanton I visited the Thrift Shop that was housed in the church. It was both a mission of the church and a substantial source of income (i.e. in 1986 it raised about five thousand dollars). Within minutes after arriving at the Thrift Shop I was asked by a woman named Doris what I thought of psychics. I could think of nothing more astute to say than, "I'm open to any form of spirituality that leads to God." Doris, it turns out, read the Tarot cards and considered her self a psychic. She even saw spiritual beings helping me when I preached.

The seminary certainly had not prepared me for dealing with psychics. It happened that there was another woman, one who came to our Sunday evening Bible study, who was also something of a psychic. She told me that she saw a purple aura around me. I later learned that purple auras are understood by some to be a sign of spirituality. I'm grateful for both of these women because they introduced me to aspects of spirituality that made me realize that my faith journey as a Christian was not the only kind that was spiritual. This lesson would later help me to be open to the various spiritual paths that the military veterans at the VA hospital in Vermont would talk about when I became their Protestant chaplain.

Barbara, the church organist, taught me a most valuable lesson while I was dealing with the various issues of Memorial United Methodist Church—one that contradicted a lesson that my father had taught me as a young boy. From my father I had learned that I must always be ready to fight. Along the way I discovered that I was better with words than with my fists. When I got to the Swanton Memorial United Methodist Church I was challenged by Barbara's loving personality to rethink whether I always had to fight back. As I noted earlier, she had suffered a displacement from her position as church organist before I arrived. She eventually was reappointed to that position. Whenever we talked about the church she spoke frankly about the politics of the church, including the loss of her position, but she was never unkind. She was both a realist about the brokenness of the church and forgiving of those who were unkind to her.

All of us at Swanton Memorial United Methodist Church learned another valuable lesson from another older lady. Her name was Margaret and she was, to say the least, candid with her opinions. I always appreciated her for her candor. One day, however, she was especially candid about something that most people don't like to discuss.

She announced in church before the service started that she was tired of going to funerals and seeing all the bouquets of flowers for people who probably never got a single flower before they died. She declared, "I want my flowers before I die!" What a gift she gave to the congregation! All of a sudden people could talk about giving and receiving flowers apart from dying and death. For the rest of the time that I was at that church each month someone would be presented with a bouquet of flowers for something they had done or just for being the person they were.

I also learned a profound lesson from my wife Jane in Swanton. She was literally inspired by God to write a play. She had no training in writing and only a little experience in theater but she created a play in which a Christ figure, played by a young woman with some dance training, came up to a series of us and mimed an offer to dance with us. All of us were supposed to be people with specific problems. I was a man in prison. When Christ came to dance with me I resisted and then I danced with her. It was one of the most amazing lessons of my life—that I could refuse to dance with Christ and s/he would still want to dance with me. Not everyone in the congregation realized how inspired that play was but I did. There is something about acting out one's refusal to "dance" with Christ that makes our choice so much more real than all of the Bible study or listening to sermons could ever make it.

PROCTORSVILLE, VERMONT:

When I was first hired as a part-time Protestant chaplain at the VA hospital in Vermont I needed a part-time position as a pastor to supplement our income. As it happened, the nearest United Methodist Church that needed a pastor was thirty-seven miles away in the little town of Proctorsville.

I was grateful both that they accepted me as their pastor and for how well they functioned as a congregation during my pastorate with them. They were a genuinely kind group of people who appreciated whatever I could do for them.

Perhaps the most generous act that we did together was to rearrange the worship service so that the children and their Sunday School teachers could attend the monthly service of Holy Communion. Many, perhaps most, churches are not known for an abundance of flexibility especially when it comes to the order of worship.

However, the people of St. James UMC wanted a change in the Communion service. So we worked together and created a way for the entire Sunday School to be together with the rest of us at the time of Communion. Instead of having the Sunday School come upstairs at the end of the service to receive what probably seemed to them as a little bit of bread and grape juice we had them all in church at the beginning of the service. We opened the service with a prayer. I read a short selection from the Bible and did a brief teaching moment with them about the meaning of that reading. Then I did the Communion prayer and invited the Sunday School to come down first. After they had received the sacrament the rest of the congregation would come forward and the Sunday School would go off to their classes. I only wish that some other congregation had expressed concern about the children and their teachers being more a part of the service of Holy Communion. I certainly never thought of it before then.

THETFORD CENTER, VT.:

I agreed to be the pastor of the Timothy Frost UMC even though I was, by then, the full-time Chief of the Chaplain Service at the Veterans Administration hospital. The church had a major issue to deal with and they were divided. It was my job to help them to face both their divisions and the feelings that went with them. Needless to say it was an intense experience but it led to a significant amount of healing during the eight months that I was there.

What was I grateful for? I was grateful for the civilized way in which we addressed the differences of opinion and the strong feelings held by both sides. They weren't happy at having to deal with the issue but they were committed to facing and finding a way though their feelings.

The second experience that I was grateful for may sound like a trivial lesson. Nevertheless, it was important and one that I had not learned anywhere else. The people of the Timothy Frost UMC taught me the importance of having a fellowship time and some food together after worship. I had been to only a few churches that had a coffee hour after worship. Most of the time people seemed to be in a hurry to get home or wherever they were going as soon as worship was done. The people of Timothy Frost UMC wanted to be together.

How did I know that? Well, again, it may sound like a small thing but the people at Timothy Frost UMC not only had coffee and pastry after worship. They had cheese! I had never been to a church that served crackers and cheese to go with their coffee hour. Somehow it said to me that this was a time to sit and visit with each other as we ate something more substantial than sugary deserts. I appreciated their emphasis on being together after worship.

There is a final lesson that I am grateful for having learned at this church. It was a lesson in self-awareness that the organist taught me. She said to me before worship one day that she had never met a person who spoke so softly and yet who could speak so forcefully while preaching. It had never occurred to me that I was soft-spoken in conversations with my parishioners. As I and many of the people with whom I interact have gotten older I monitor my voice more carefully so that I speak loudly enough.

SEARSPORT, ME.:

I served these two churches on the coast of Maine after I had retired both from the VA hospital and from full-time ministry as a United Methodist minister. Like the last parish that I served in Vermont, they, too, were dealing with strong feelings. They weren't divided. Instead, they were united in their grief that their pastor had become so ill that he had to retire from ministry. Then he died shortly after retiring. So, my task, besides carrying out the usual duties of a pastor, was to help them to grieve. I did that and I was grateful for the opportunity to do so.

While serving these two congregations, I also learned a lesson from the organist at North Searsport UMC (organists have a lot to share in the average church). Again, it was another one of those lessons that did not appear in the seminary curriculum. Frank was his name and he was an excellent piano player. He was so good that he had a job that began at 10:30 a.m. in a resort that was probably an hour's drive away. The service started at 8:45 a.m. and it was understood by the congregation that Frank would leave at 9:30 a.m.—not a minute later. The same order of worship that took an hour or more in the later service in Searsport UMC was done in forty-five minutes at North Searsport UMC. Frank would drop a verse of a hymn and play the other verses faster than I had ever heard anyone play in church. I learned, quite simply, that a sixty-minute service could be done in forty-five minutes without upsetting anyone. More importantly, I learned that a congregation could accommodate the needs of someone they cared about.

POST-RETIREMENT SUPPLY PREACHING:

One final lesson from Northern New England churches came in the form of affirmation. After I retired from the VA hospital in Vermont I supply preached at eleven churches in Maine. I was simply amazed and grateful for their acceptance of me as their substitute worship leader. It didn't seem to matter what their denominational affiliation was. They were affirming of my preaching and worship leadership.

Since moving to California in early 2008 I have had the same experience when I supply preach. It is wonderful to be accepted and I am grateful for everyone's kindness.

CHAPTER 7
—VETERANS AND HOSPITAL STAFF

INTRODUCTION:

The twelve years that I worked at the VA hospital in Vermont were an entirely different kind of ministry than pastoring local churches. For one thing, life and death issues were a daily, sometimes several times daily, occurrence. For another, I was not the only professional person who was trying to help the patients. I had a staff of two part-time chaplains as well as pastors who would be on call for emergencies and for leading chapel worship periodically. We worked with literally hundreds of nurses, physicians and other medical and support staff to make the hospital as much of a healing environment as possible.

Unlike the people that I knew in the churches in Maine and Vermont, every patient and many of the staff were veterans of the military. They had unique spiritual needs and many of their physical, emotional and social needs were challenging as well. Unlike non-VA hospitals all of our patients had been taught to kill and many of those who had been in combat still were easily startled. Without realizing what they were doing they might awaken ready to defend themselves from what seemed to be a danger. I used to tell student chaplains that they should never awaken a sleeping veteran by touching them, no matter how gently, and they should never approach a veteran from behind. Like many other lessons I had to learn this on the job.

The majority of veterans were different from my previous parishioners in another way. Most of them were only in the hospital for relatively short periods of time—days to weeks. So, ministry was mostly in the form of crisis ministry. Long, leisurely visits in a home setting were not possible. The exceptions were the patients who were in the Nursing Home Care Unit (NHCU) and in the psychiatric unit. Many of the NHCU patients had been there for years and I had the opportunity to visit them regularly and lead Bible study groups with them. The patients on the psychiatric ward often returned for treatment and I got to know many of them over a period of years.

The people at the VA hospital taught me a different set of lessons than any other group. They helped me to learn how to minister to men and women who had been affected, sometimes profoundly and even traumatically, by their experiences in the military. None of this was covered in my seminary education or in my counseling training. What I describe in the rest of this chapter are some of the areas where I had the most to learn and I am grateful for every person who helped me to learn these lessons.

BOUNDARIES:

Boundaries were an important issue for veterans. Most of the veterans whom I met, numbering in the thousands, allowed me to visit them because I identified myself as a chaplain. For most of the time I was at the VA hospital I did that verbally and also non-verbally (i.e. I wore a clergy shirt and a cross). Most of them had positive memories of chaplains in the military.

However, not all veterans were in the mood for a visit from a chaplain. Early in my career as a chaplain at the VA hospital in Vermont I entered a room on a medical ward for what I thought was a routine visit. I was making the rounds in the four bed ward when I attempted to engage an older gentleman who, it turned out, didn't want to talk with me. He made this clear first by telling me so. Then, when I turned to the patient in the next bed (i.e. I didn't leave the room immediately even though I did stop talking to the man who was upset) he picked up his breakfast plate and threatened to throw it at me unless I left the room immediately. Needless to say, I learned to leave when someone told me they didn't want to talk with me.

I learned that I might have no warning that a person was upset with me. During a group on spiritual issues a veteran stood up and began yelling at me. What he said didn't matter as much as the fact that he advanced towards me in a menacing way. I stood perfectly still and waited for him to finish. I didn't contradict him and I didn't attempt to touch him. To do so might have triggered an assault by this man who was overwhelmed by what appeared to be a conflict between his religious values and something that I said or something that I represented as a chaplain. In the years to come he decided to trust me and never acted in an angry or threatening manner with me again. In fact, the last time that we met he was quite concerned about my well-being.

Another veteran, one with severe Post Traumatic Stress Disorder and Chronic Depression, told me years after I first met him about his first experience with me. It had to do with my respecting his boundaries. When I came into his room I introduced myself and asked if I could help.

He politely but clearly told me that this was not a good time. I gave him my card and said that I would be available whenever he wanted to talk. We eventually talked and he attended groups that I led on spiritual issues many times. He even asked me to officiate at his wedding. It was fortunate for me that other veterans had already taught me the importance of respecting patients' boundaries.

On another occasion I went to the psychiatric ward where a veteran was attempting to leave against medical advice. The protocol at that time was to call a special code throughout the hospital which would alert about fifteen or twenty people to come to constitute a presence, not a force, in support of the staff on the affected ward. I would come intending my presence to be a sign of God's presence in the midst of whatever chaos was going on.

I arrived one day to find Bill inching his way out of the psychiatric ward amidst a large group of staff. Finally, two VA police officers arrived and restrained him but only with a great deal of effort. While all of this was going on Bill looked at me and said, "Larry, you don't want to be part of this!" It was a warning and I heard it. I stayed back and simply assured him that I was there for him as well as the staff. I knew that if I interfered he would have turned on me even though, when he wasn't upset, he liked me a lot. I was grateful that he was clear about his boundaries.

HUMOR:

On the more amusing side, there was an older man in the NHCU named Joe. He suffered from rheumatoid arthritis but he never complained. For that matter, Joe always had a sense of humor. One of his favorite ways to have fun happened as he sat in the doorway to his room while I stood out in the hallway talking to him. He sat in his doorway so that he could see what was happening in the ward. He always waited until one of the senior people in the administration of the hospital was coming down the hall. Then he would yell out, "Help! Help! The Reverend is picking on me!" I learned that even when in pain at least some people can choose to have a sense of humor.

SUFFERING:

There are lessons to be learned about suffering that are specific to veterans. Another one of the veterans on the NHCU was named Raymond. Ray was a combat veteran from World War II who served in the South Pacific. He was very appreciative of my visits and was always willing to have me pray with him. But he would never discuss his experiences in combat with me. He would only hint at them saying, with great sadness in his voice and on his face, "Reverend, you wouldn't believe! You wouldn't believe!" Whatever Ray saw or did was too terrible, at least in his mind, to share even with me. Suffering is sometimes so awful that veterans believe that it can never be shared.

More than one of the men who were dying from cancer taught me about a sense of guilt that didn't seem to have anything to do with what actually happened in their lives. In an attempt to make sense out of their suffering they would often say, "I must have done something awful to deserve this much pain!" They could not believe that God would allow them to suffer that much unless they had done something to deserve it. Nor, frankly, was I able to explain why they suffered so much. Mostly, I learned to listen and, whenever I thought that they could stand to hear it, I assured them of God's love. Often they would allow me to pray with them.

Herb, on the other hand, knew exactly why he was a quadriplegic. He had returned from the military relatively unscathed except for a tendency to drink too much and drive too fast. One night he rounded a curve at about 120 miles per hour and lost control of his car.

He never complained. He was always happy and enjoyed jokes. Herb wasn't bitter in the least as far as I could tell. Of course, I met him years after the accident and he had had a great deal of time to adjust. But, he had adjusted! I watched in amazement as he and at least some of the other veterans coped with their disabling conditions.

Amongst the most difficult forms of suffering to understand is the spiritual and emotional pain caused by trauma—including trauma in the military. Many veterans with Post Traumatic Stress Disorder, as well as other psychiatric disorders, shared their memories and feelings as I visited them or led them in groups that focused on the spiritual dimensions of suffering.

One was named Bob. We had talked many times about his memories and we would continue to talk about them for years. However, there was one day in particular when Bob asked me to come into the chapel with him. I thought that he wanted me to pray with him. It was fortunate that no one else wanted to use the chapel while we were in there because Bob was distraught over the memories that he could no longer escape.

He had given up drinking some years ago. Prior to that point, drinking large quantities of alcohol had been the only way that he could suppress his memories from his experiences in the military. When he came to the VA hospital he received psychiatric care including medications. But they couldn't heal his spiritual and emotional pain.

As we sat in the chapel he poured out his memories and sobbed—sometimes loudly. There was no way that I could console him. All I could do was to listen until he was ready for a prayer. That day was one of the days that I was reminded, that being present and listening was sometimes all that I could do for a suffering veteran. At the same time I was reminded that it was indeed very important for me to listen. When Bob was finished he gave me a small metal angel that he had carried for several years. It was his way of thanking me and perhaps symbolizing his trust in me. I learned to tell the student chaplains to "listen and care" when they visited the veterans.

CONFESSION:

I am not now and never have been a Catholic priest. However, I was approached by a few veterans who asked if I would hear their confessions. I always told them that I wasn't a Catholic priest and I would remind them that we had a Catholic priest on our staff. However, a few veterans wanted me to hear their confessions and I did. It is a humbling experience to have someone trust you with their sins.

I didn't believe that I had the authority to forgive anyone's sin unless that person had offended me. However, after hearing the veteran's confession I always prayed both for him (Yes, these were all men.) to be forgiven and for him to be able to accept God's mercy. The veterans taught, or perhaps reminded me, that denominational differences are less important than whether the chaplain was willing to listen and care.

All too often, however, I encountered veterans who never got to the stage of being ready to confess because they believed that even God could not forgive what they had done. The gift in this kind of experience is in being allowed into the soul of a person who cannot believe that God would come to them lovingly. Yet they allow one of God's representatives to come and, in that, there is hope of healing.

DYING AND DEATH:

I've met a lot of people as a pastor who spent a great deal of energy denying the reality of death. Many are afraid of dying and death. The veterans taught me that death is not to be feared. In many instances it is welcomed as a release from a lifetime of suffering. I learned that the veterans who had been in combat had long ago faced their fears of dying.

Early in my career as a veterans' chaplain I faced my limits in knowing what to do for a dying veteran. He was a young marine, 38 years old, and his girlfriend and family came to me because they did not know how to help him to die peacefully. Everyone knew he was dying including the patient. But he seemed unable to "let go" and die peacefully.

I listened to his family and friends and went in to talk with him. He said very little. However, I learned that he had a Christian background. So, after reading from the Bible, especially Psalm 23, and saying some prayers with him I decided to sing the children's hymn, "Jesus Loves Me." The words to the first verse are, "Jesus loves me, this I know, for the Bible tells me so; little ones to him belong, they are weak but he is strong. Yes, Jesus loves me, Yes, Jesus loves me, Yes, Jesus loves me, the Bible tells me so."

It was all I could think to do for him. I reasoned that perhaps the hymn might reach him where spoken words wouldn't. I thought that it might take him back to an earlier time in his life when he was less afraid.

I also recommended to the family that they take breaks from standing by his bedside so that he could be alone for a little while. Several veterans, by the way they died, showed me that some people want to die alone—perhaps to spare their loved ones from the stress of seeing them die. This young man did, in fact, die early the next morning while his family was getting coffee. It may seem strange that absence can be the greatest gift that one can give but, if the dying person wants to spare us what they think might be the burden of watching them die, then it is the gift that we should be willing to receive. It was one more lesson that the veterans helped me to learn.

Another gift that I received in ministry with veterans came as I watched the courage shown by a 48 year-old dying veteran and his family. He and his wife had a nine year-old daughter. Her mother brought her in to say "Goodbye" to her father and I was there. It was all that I could do not to break down and cry as I saw this father bid farewell to his daughter. His wife took her out after several minutes. He died two hours later.

Another lesson about dying that I learned came in the form of two people who had no faith of any sort. The veteran was in his early thirties and he and his wife had two young sons. The nurses asked the chaplains to visit to help them to cope first with the uncertainty about what was wrong with the veteran and then with his terminal diagnosis. Despite all my training I could find nothing to build on to help them with their very understandable depression. I asked the other two chaplains to go in to visit them but they were likewise unable to find common ground with the family.

Yet, the family must have decided to trust me. Although I didn't think that I was accomplishing anything, the widow asked me to officiate at her husband's memorial service in the VA chapel. I appreciated her trust in me and in a God that probably seemed pretty remote to her at that moment. Later, both she and her sons attended the church where Jane and I worshipped.

Another lesson has to do with people in love and how they often want to show the world that they are in love. I've been privileged to officiate at dozens of weddings both as a church pastor and as a VA chaplain. One of the more moving weddings that I officiated at happened in the intensive care unit. A gentleman in his late seventies was very ill and not expected to live more than a few days. He had lived with a woman for many years and they wanted to get married but he could not leave the intensive care unit to be married in the chapel. So, we did the wedding in the patient's room. Two hospital volunteers served as witnesses and two nurses and a physician were also present. The dietary department baked a small wedding cake and we celebrated their commitment to each other. It was a lesson for me in the power of life-long love wanting to demonstrate how real it is even in the face of imminent death. It was also a reminder of the great privilege that chaplains and others who care for the sick and the dying are given when we are allowed into their lives.

The other gift that I received from dying veterans was to actually be present when the person died. It happened dozens of times during my tenure as a chaplain. Never was it a frightening experience. Never was it anything but a peaceful passing of the person's spirit from this plane of existence to what I believe is a higher plane of existence. In large measure, this peaceful death process was enabled by the good care that the nursing and medical staff provided to patients and their families. I am grateful for each peaceful death that I was able to witness. Each one helped me to realize that death is not to be feared. It is a normal transition in life.

Another veteran taught me a different kind of lesson about what love would endure for the sake of the beloved. The veteran was a man in his sixties and he had married a younger woman. In fact, I had officiated at the wedding. Then the veteran developed a terminal illness. He did something remarkable. He asked the physicians to do everything that they could to keep him alive for a year! In those days a widow could not qualify for a social security pension based on her husband's income unless they had been married for a year. They had been married only a month or two when he was diagnosed with cancer. The veteran wasn't holding on for a cure. Nor did he have any false hopes of having any reasonably quality of life. In fact, his quality of life quickly became marginal. Sadly, he died a few weeks later. What amazed me was that he was willing to endure whatever he had to undergo to stay alive so that his wife would get a pension for her and her child.

PHYSICIANS:

Physicians have taught me many lessons but one of the most valuable came during an ethics consultation. The Ethics Advisory Committee (EAC) at the VA hospital in Vermont had been asked to consult about what level of care a very ill man should have. I visited him as a member of the EAC but I was wearing a clergy shirt—my standard way to be identified as a chaplain in that hospital. I did my best to find out what the patient wanted for his care but at the end of the discussion he seemed to be comfortable with not having what we used to refer to as "extraordinary care" to prolong his life. The physician, however, had gotten a different answer from the patient and was understandably confused when I reported what the patient had said to me. The physician then pointed out to me, "Look at what you have to offer the patient—life in heaven! Look at what little I have to offer!" We went back to the patient together and, with us both present, the patient was able to decide that he wanted the extra medical care that the physician was offering him.

In a way, this was not a new lesson. Many times both I and my staff had noticed what happened when a physician entered a patient room. No matter who was talking to the patient, whether a nurse, chaplain, family member or some other visitor, the patient's attention immediately shifted to the physician when s/he entered the room. The reality was and is that the patients want and need to hear from their doctors. It is a reminder that most of us continue to hope that life will continue for as long as possible and, when it is clear that it will end, that it will do so as comfortably as possible. Physicians can do a great deal to extend life and, with the help of the nurses and allied healthcare staff, make it as comfortable as possible.

The other lesson that I learned from physicians at the VA hospital was how many of them were open to the spiritual dimension of the patients' experiences. My observations of a patient's spiritual well-being and spiritual needs were welcomed in the patients' charts. The insights of the chaplaincy staff were routinely solicited at the VA hospital by medical, nursing and allied healthcare professionals. I was invited to speak on spiritual issues in the VA department of psychiatry meetings and I was appointed an instructor in the Dartmouth Medical School department of psychiatry.

I am grateful to the resident and staff physicians for their trust in me as a chaplain and as an ethicist. I am particularly grateful for their openness to my leadership of the monthly ethics rounds. They helped me to discover how we could work together to help the veterans and their loved ones.

CONCLUSION

Somewhere in my reading about counseling techniques I encountered a method for helping a person to heal from spiritual and emotional harm. This can be done with a counselor or by oneself. I have used it many times to help in my recovery from the darker parts of my life.

It involves remembering a scene in which something bad happened to yourself. As we bring that scene into focus in our mind we then invite Jesus (if we are Christian or open to Jesus' presence in our lives) to come into that scene and to stay there. After we do that for as many unpleasant or even traumatic memories as we can recall there is a gradual shift in our inner experience. Instead of being people who live with memories of suffering we become people who live with the assurance that Jesus is in every experience of suffering that we have. In other words, we are not alone—even in our darkest moments. God is with us wherever we are.

One of the other ways that I know that God is with me is the presence of all the good people that God has sent to be part of my life. I have truly been blessed to know so many good people who have given so much to help me to become more of the person that God wants me to be.

I continue to be blessed by good people in what may be the final chapter(s) of my life here in California. Some of them are people I meet mostly in church while others are neighbors or friends we have met in other places. Many are family. Some are friends whom we connect with mostly through telephone calls, letters and e-mail. I feel blessed by all of them.

Most of all, I am grateful for what my wife, Jane, has brought and continues to bring into my life. I simply cannot imagine what my life would have been like without her. She is God's greatest gift to me and I'm sure that others who know her regard her as a real blessing in their lives as well.

www.ingramcontent.com/pod-product-compliance
Lightning Source LLC
LaVergne TN
LVHW040152080526
838202LV00042B/3133